# Estate Planning
## through Family Meetings
### (without breaking up the family)

Lynne Butler, BA, LLB

D1441613

**Self-Counsel Press Inc.**
(*a subsidiary of*)
International Self-Counsel Press Ltd.
USA     Canada

*Self-Counsel Press acknowledges the financial support of the Government of Canada through the Canada Book Fund (CBF) for our publishing activities.*

*Printed in Canada.*

*First edition: 2010*

**Library and Archives Canada Cataloguing in Publication**

Butler, Lynne

     Estate Planning through family meetings / Lynne Butler.

ISBN 978-1-77040-036-8

    1. Estate planning.  2. Communication in families.  3. Adult children of aging parents — Family relationships.  I. Title.

| | | |
|---|---|---|
| K4568.B88 2010 | 346.05'2 | C2009-906328-X |

Inside Image

Copyright©iStockphoto/Adult Students Studying/Monkey Business Images
Copyright©iStockphoto/Old-Fashioned Will and Testament/Monkey Business Images
Copyright©iStockphoto/Business Signature/riccardocova

**Self-Counsel Press Inc.**
*(a subsidiary of)*
International Self-Counsel Press Ltd.

| | |
|---|---|
| 1704 North State Street | 1481 Charlotte Road |
| Bellingham, WA 98225 | North Vancouver, BC  V7J 1H1 |
| USA | Canada |

*This book is dedicated to Chelsea for her encouragement and love,*
*and for being the best daughter and friend I could possibly have.*

# Contents

# Notice to Readers

# Introduction

Have you ever tried to bring up a sensitive topic with someone who simply did not want to talk about it? You feel like you have to force a conversation on someone because you really think he or she needs to know something important, but it seems impossible. The person is unhappy about it and you are uncomfortable and the whole thing ends up being an argument or creating a scene. Almost everyone has been in that situation once or twice, and almost everyone wishes they knew a better way to deal with it.

Talking to your parents about difficult topics has an extra dimension of difficulty simply because they are your parents. Most of us were raised to respect our parents and not to question their judgment about how they live their lives. It can be a lot easier for a parent to shut down an unwanted conversation than it is for other people, just by drawing on authority as your mother or father.

In addition, most of us have trouble making the shift from having our parents look after us to having us look after our parents. We are so used to thinking of them as being competent individuals that it is difficult to accept that they may need our help. This can make many people reluctant to speak up on sensitive topics, and we may wait too long to take on the role of protector.

Have you ever tried to tell your aging parents that you think they might be losing their mental faculties and that legal steps should be taken to let someone take over? That is an unpleasant conversation that many people dread, as it rarely goes well. Then there is the talk in which you try to convince your aging parents that they need to make wills. Again, this topic is near the top of the list of what everyone wants to avoid.

What about holding a family meeting? It is a great idea in principle but most families have never had one. They might feel awkward trying to hold one. Just the idea of having this kind of meeting raises a flurry of questions for most people, such as who should go to the family meeting? Who should run the meeting? What should be talked about in the meeting? The biggest question of all is how do you turn the results of a family meeting into a legally effective estate plan?

How do you have this conversation with your parents? How do you get the whole family to talk about what needs to be done for your mom and dad? How do you make sure that all of the talking is worthwhile and results in a proper, legally documented, sensible estate plan?

Knowing that the topic is essential does not necessarily make it any easier to bring up.

This book will explore how and when to raise these topics in a constructive way and bring about a successful discussion. The goal is to clarify and understand your parents' or your family's goals and document them in a legally effective way. Whether you just want to talk to your parents or you want to hold a full family conference, you will find ideas in this book about how to handle it in a way that will result in the right legal solution being put into place.

If you are reading this book, you may have a parent or other relative who is ill, in need of surgery, contemplating a move to long-term care, or showing the early signs of mental deterioration. In other words, your parent is beginning to need help from you and other family members. Most likely, the parent you are concerned about does not have a will, an enduring power of attorney, or a health-care directive in place. You want your parent to get these documents in place before it is too late.

Even if your parents are completely healthy and are showing no signs yet of failing mental capacity or physical frailty, you may rightly want them to get on with their planning while they are mentally healthy. The topics covered in this book apply equally to elderly individuals who still have their complete mental and physical health.

Maybe you are thinking about how to bring up the subject of planning with your parents, or you have already brought it up and did not get the reaction you hoped for. Perhaps they were reluctant to do any planning, or even worse, they saw your involvement as interference and resent you for it.

Now what? How do you start a constructive conversation on such a potentially upsetting subject? Who should be involved? What is the process going to be like? How do you get things going without causing any family disharmony or upsetting anyone? Can it possibly be done without tears or shouting? What can you reasonably expect to achieve? Is it really possible to take all of this emotion and talking and form it into a legal plan of action that will be in place when you need it?

In this book we will explore all of these questions, and more. You will learn more about why people are reluctant to plan, so that you can understand and deal with objections to planning. You will read about some specific conversation starters for bringing up a touchy legal subject with your parents or with the entire extended family. You will see how family meetings are held and will learn to design an agenda for your own meeting. You will learn more about who should be included and excluded. You will also learn more about some of the specific situations and questions that cause problems for family estate planning as well as ideas for dealing with them.

There are two different situations addressed throughout the chapters of this book. One is the case in which you want to speak only to your parents and there is nobody else in the family who will be involved in the process. This is where many readers will see a familiar scenario. Chapter 4 talks specifically about having a conversation with parents, though the information in all chapters will be useful to help you prepare for, conduct, and follow up on your discussion.

The second situation is that in which an entire family is going to sit down together to decide what needs to be done. This might be to talk about a parent's failing health and what the family should do about it. The family might sit down to talk together where there is a family business, farm, or cottage to deal with. Sometimes families like to do communal planning not because of a business or cottage, but because they want to ensure that family wealth is preserved or distributed fairly. Sometimes a family meeting is held simply because having such a meeting will ensure that everyone knows what is happening and individual family members will have the chance to be involved in decision making. Quite often the parents want a family meeting just because they want to know what everyone thinks of their plans.

Chapter 8 will show you how to prepare an agenda. Chapters 8, 9, and 10 will help you run your meeting successfully and smoothly. Chapter 11 will help you with the matters that have to be taken care of after the discussions have taken place.

If you are using professional advisors such as lawyers and accountants, you will find that this book gives you plenty of practical tips and ideas about making the most of the information you are receiving from those advisors. It will bring up topics that interest you and that you will want to explore further with your professional advisors. It will also give you ideas on how and when to involve your lawyer or accountant.

This book will also talk about the human side of making legal arrangements; it explores the fears and superstitions that hinder estate planning and gives you ideas for dealing with them. It will help you remember that though legal questions are being raised, there are real people with real fears and feelings involved at every stage. This book will be a useful supplement to the advice you are getting from other sources.

This book also comes with a CD that includes forms that you can use to gather your thoughts about the various legal solutions offered so that you can put what you have learned to work. It takes a practical, hands-on approach that is designed to help you get moving, get your parents and family moving, and reach your estate-planning goals.

Documents that have more or less the same legal effect have different names in different geographic locations. This is because laws having to do with wills, probate, and incapacity are almost all made at the local level, as opposed to the federal level. In this book we use the terms "Enduring Power of Attorney" and "Health-Care Directive" but those documents are known by other names as well, as the following two lists will show. These lists should help you relate the information you see in this book to the information you hear or read about locally from lawyers, accountants, in magazines, or other sources.

Enduring Power of Attorney is also known as the following:

- Continuing Power of Attorney
- Durable Power of Attorney
- Lasting Power of Attorney
- Mandate Given in Anticipation of Incapacity
- Power of Attorney for Property

Note that in this book, the word "attorney" does not refer to a lawyer.

Health-Care Directive is also known as the following:

- Advance Directive
- Advance Health-Care Directive
- Durable Power of Attorney for Health Care
- Health-Care Proxy
- Living Will
- Patient Advocate Designation
- Personal-Care Power of Attorney
- Personal Directive
- Power of Attorney for Personal Care

# Addressing
# Difficult Topics

It is not really surprising that people do not want to talk about making their wills. Planning a will forces people to think about their own mortality. We all know that one day we will pass away, but most people do not want to think about that if they can help it. The reluctance to talk about it only increases when someone is terminally ill or critically injured, because the possibility of losing a loved one is uncomfortably close.

Talking about planning for possible mental incapacity is even harder. The fact is, our population is aging. The baby boomer generation is nearing retirement age. The parents of the boomers are now elderly. People live longer now than they ever have, thanks to medical and technological advancements. Living longer, though, does not necessarily mean living your whole life with full mental and physical abilities intact. This is where the planning becomes important and the topic becomes touchy.

The knowledge that one day a parent could have to live with mental or physical impairment leaves many of us in a difficult situation in which we know we should take action, and we are willing to take action, but we are not sure how to do what we need to do. Many people have brought up subjects like moving a parent to a long-term care facility, helping out with banking, or making wills with sincere concern for an aging relative, only to find that their concern is unwelcome. The parents do not always want to do any planning, or even talk about it. The well-intentioned person is shut down, no help is accepted by the parents, and to top it all off, now there is resentment or tension between family members.

With this in mind, you may have come to the realization that your parents or other aging relatives need do some planning while they are still healthy. Or, it might have become painfully obvious to you that a parent is struggling with the onset of physical illness or mental lapses due to the process of aging. With their best interests at heart, you may ask your parents whether the necessary documents have been done. If you have asked this question, you may have discovered that your parents have no legal paperwork or inadequate paperwork in place. Most people fail to prepare the legal documents they need. With the onset of illness or dementia, the time for preparation of documents is running out.

# 1. Troublesome Topics That Need to Be Discussed

Everyone is different so there is no way to predict every subject that is going to upset every person. However, there are some specific topics that are almost always hard to talk about and which are of special interest to aging parents and their families. These topics are mental capacity, money, and will planning. Each of these can be problematic for a family, sometimes extremely so, but finding the right legal solution will resolve those problems to a large extent.

Finding the right legal solution does not necessarily involve putting sweeping changes into place immediately; it means understanding the problem and having a plan in place to deal with it when the need arises. It means knowing in advance who is ready and willing to take on responsibilities for other people. It means having the right paperwork in place so that when medical or financial crises occur, they are not made worse by delays, challenges, or requests for clarification.

The topics mentioned in this section — mental incapacity, money and insurance, and will planning — will be the main focus of this book. They are the subjects that will be referred to in later chapters, which talk about holding a conversation with your parents or a meeting with your family. You will notice that although these topics are listed separately here, in real life they overlap and blend together. This means that the legal solutions to deal with them may also overlap.

## 1.1 Mental incapacity

Mental capacity is the ability to make reasonable decisions. What is considered "reasonable" can be open to interpretation, but most people would consider a decision reasonable if it takes into account all relevant factors known to the decision maker, and takes into account the possible consequences of the decision.

For example, most of us would consider giving a cash donation to a charity a reasonable decision, but not if the donation was so large that it left the giver no money to pay for rent or food. A person who did not realize that giving his or her money away would cause financial hardship for himself or herself would probably lack mental capacity, particularly if this inability to manage money was a long-term pattern.

A decision is not considered reasonable if it is forced on a person by way of verbal threat or physical intimidation. It is not reasonable if it needlessly harms the person or his or her family members who are dependent on him or her.

A decision does not have to be popular to be reasonable, which is an important point when it comes to mental capacity. Every one of us has at some time made a financial decision that made someone around us unhappy, such as overspending on a gift, or buying something frivolous. That is simply human nature to make the occasional poorly thought out, impulsive decision, particularly among younger people.

However, it is not uncommon for the adult children of an aging person to be unhappy with the decisions being made by their parent, particularly financial decisions. Sometimes this leads the children to attempt to use the legal system to control or stop the parent's financial independence. This is where it becomes necessary to tell the difference between, on one hand, a parent who cannot make good financial choices and, on the other hand, a parent who can make good financial choices but whose choices are somewhat unusual.

For example, a person who continually buys cans of dog food that are simply stored by the case in the basement because he or she does not remember that he or she does not have a dog is not making good financial choices. On the other hand, a person who takes skydiving lessons four times a week might seem odd to you but is, on the face of it, making a good choice of how to spend his or her money.

The fact that your parent makes a decision that you do not like or agree with does not mean that your parent has lost mental capacity. It is his or her money after all. Your aging parent is free to make as many unpopular decisions as he or she wishes, as long as those decisions are not the result of poor memory, confusion, or pressure by another person.

You might notice that your mom or dad is beginning to forget things and fails to recognize people. He or she can no longer take care of familiar tasks such as cooking, driving, or gardening that he or she used to be able to do easily. The person cannot keep track of money and does not know which bills have been paid and which have not. You are pretty sure your parent is not taking his or her prescribed medications properly. You may have no choice but to conclude that your parent is beginning to lose mental capacity. You think it is time for your parent to let someone else help him or her.

Noticing that there is a possible problem with mental capacity is the easy part, and just the beginning of what might be a long, emotionally draining experience. Telling your mother or father that you think he or she is losing mental capacity and needs help is possibly the hardest conversation you will ever have. Most (but not all) parents will fight to retain independence and privacy. If you have seen the beginning of this deterioration in your parent, it can be almost impossible to raise the topic without insulting, frightening, or upsetting the person. Once the deterioration has gone past the initial stages, talking about it becomes infinitely more upsetting for everyone involved.

Alzheimer's disease, other dementias, illnesses, and physical deterioration may all contribute to the eventual lessening of an individual's ability to look after his or her own decisions. The pace at which changes occur is different in every individual. Sometimes this means that there is a span of several months, or even years, during which an individual is not capable of making good decisions alone and needs help from others.

As the family member of someone who is losing capacity, your goal is to assess the problem and offer the assistance that is wanted and needed. You may discover that although help is needed, it is not always wanted by your parent. It can be really difficult to persuade your parent to let you help or to allow you to find others to help. Because there is so much at stake in the parent's view — such as independence, identity, freedom, dignity, and privacy — the discussion can become very emotional.

Just as we should all plan for our eventual passing away by preparing a will that sets out our wishes, we should all plan for the possibility that we might lose our mental faculties as we age. We need to prepare legal documents that name individuals to make decisions for us if we cannot do that for ourselves any longer.

All aging individuals should have these planning documents in place but it is a very delicate topic. Most people realize that as they lose their mental abilities, they might also be losing their independence, dignity, and privacy. This idea is disturbing and alarming to most elderly people. Nobody wants to believe it is happening to them, and when it is happening, it is disorienting and frightening. Because we do not want to upset anyone, we do not bring up the topic, leaving our elderly family members without the help they need.

## 1.2 Money and insurance

The problem with talking to your parents about money is that it is hard not to appear greedy, either to them or to other family members who find out you have raised the subject. Most people are more private about their finances than they are about any other aspect of their lives. You might ask your parent, "Have you got your money invested safely and properly?" and what they hear might be, "How much money do you have, and are you leaving it to me when you pass away?" Money is a touchy subject.

Part of talking about money is talking about insurance. The types of insurance that are particularly relevant to aging parents and family estate planning are life insurance, long-term care insurance, and critical illness insurance (each of which is defined below). Not everyone has or needs all of these types of policies, as everybody's situation is different. However, if you are helping your parents with planning, it

is essential that you find out and understand what your parents have in place.

Insurance can be remarkably useful in filling money gaps in estates. Your parents might find it useful to meet with an insurance representative to talk about how different kinds of insurance might be helpful in their situation. You should be aware though, that it is possible to be over-insured, so your parents should thoroughly understand what a policy is going to do for them before they buy a new one.

*Life insurance* pays out an agreed-upon amount of money to a named beneficiary when the insured person dies. Often, the named beneficiary is a spouse or other family member, but life insurance can be useful when the named beneficiary is the estate of the deceased person, because this creates cash flow that did not exist before the death. Life insurance is also used frequently in conjunction with privately owned businesses to buy back the shares of a business owner who passes away.

*Long-term care insurance* covers the costs of living in a long-term care facility, or, in some cases, the costs of receiving specialized care at home. It is intended to be used by individuals who are no longer able to deal with personal care such as bathing, toileting, or meal preparation due to the complications of aging. It is paid in the form of weekly or monthly benefits and can be used to supplement government or private sources of retirement funding.

*Critical illness insurance* pays out a lump sum of money to a policy owner who suffers a major illness such as cancer or a heart attack and survives.

The fact that these types of insurance are listed here does not mean that everyone reading this book should urge their parents to buy all of these policies. They are listed so that when you have a discussion with your parents or a family meeting, you will be sure to ask what is in place. You might also see how one of these types of insurance might fill a need for the future and want to raise it at your meeting. Sometimes putting insurance to good use requires the cooperation of the whole family, such as when a group of siblings pays the premiums on a long-term care insurance policy for their parents.

The most common of all of these is life insurance. When talking about a life insurance policy, you must understand the following information about the policy:

- Who is the owner of the policy?

- Whose life is insured by the policy? (Note that some policies insure more than one life, such as Joint and Last to Die policies.)

- Who is the beneficiary of the policy (i.e., who will get the money on the death of the life-insured person)?

- Is the policy whole life, term, group, etc.?

- What is the face value of the policy (i.e., how much money will be paid out on the death of the insured person)?

## 1.3 Wills and dying

Most of us are not comfortable talking about dying, at least not about the deaths of our loved ones or ourselves. Almost nobody is comfortable asking their parents whether the parents have made wills. It is even harder to talk about wills if the parent is ill or hospitalized. Bringing up financial or legal questions when a person is dying or extremely ill may make you look cold or unfeeling to others who are distressed by the person's illness. You are not alone in finding that this is an extremely sensitive topic.

Yet, as sensitive as the topic may be, everyone is better off if it is brought up and dealt with properly.

One of the first major decisions that will be made by your parent when making a will is the choice of *executor*. This term refers to the person or people who will be in charge of your parent's estate when your parent dies. The executor's job includes everything from making funeral arrangements and paying bills to settling claims and paying out the estate to the beneficiaries.

It is common for a married couple to appoint each other as executors, but do not assume that is the case for your parents without asking. Even if they do appoint each other as their first choice, one of them is probably going to outlive the other except in very unusual circumstances. Therefore, it is also necessary for them to appoint an alternate choice of executor to take over in case the other spouse is already gone.

Should one of your parents die, the surviving parent is not always a good choice of executor and the family members should be realistic as to the capabilities and wishes of each parent.

The surviving person might not be a good choice for the job of executor if —

- he or she is beginning to show signs of mental incapacity, memory loss, or confusion;

- he or she is not the one who looked after the family's finances and has no familiarity with financial matters;

- he or she is overwhelmed, or likely to be overwhelmed, by emotions at the loss of his or her spouse;

- the parent who died owned a business that the other parent was not involved in;

- the surviving parent was the second (or subsequent) spouse of the parent who died, and the estate is going to involve the first spouse in some way; and

- he or she simply does not want to do it.

During the estate-planning process your parent can ask his or her lawyer for ideas about who should be the executor. There are plenty of possibilities, such as having one of the children act jointly along with the surviving parent or instead of the parent. Another choice is using a trust company, which is particularly suitable if there are likely to be family squabbles or disputes that will require a neutral third party as executor, or where none of the family members live close to the parents.

Whoever is chosen as executor should be aware that he or she has been appointed. If your parents want to appoint you or one of your siblings, they should let you know before they sign their wills. This is something that can be talked about at a family meeting.

A wills discussion will also cover the *distribution* of the estate, which refers to who will inherit the parents' assets after they pass away. This is, of course, where most of the disputes arise with estates, and it is an area in which many parents take great care to craft an arrangement that is fair to everyone, in their view.

In some families the distribution can be as simple as dividing whatever money is left equally among the children, but it is not always that easy. One of the most important elements of the distribution of an estate is that of special situations that need more attention than most. These situations might include a family member who is disabled and must have his or her inheritance placed in a trust, a business that is being passed down to the next generation

in the family, or a blended family that must balance the needs of a new spouse against those of the children from a previous marriage.

## 2. Are You the Right Person to Bring up the Troublesome Topics?

An issue that a number of people wrestle with is whether they *should* be giving their parents any planning advice or asking them about personal documents. Are they sticking their noses into private matters if they decide to speak up? Are they the best person to bring up the subject with the parents? If so, where do suggestion and encouragement end and where do interference and influence begin? If not them, who else is going to bring it up and see that essential documents are done? Nobody wants to be accused by siblings or other family members of trying to force a parent's hand.

What if there is a family business and nobody has been named as the person who will take over if your parent becomes ill or mentally incapable of running the business? What if your parents own a cottage that is used by all family members and it is not clear who should be able to continue using it after your parents' death and who should pay for its upkeep? What if you have a sibling who is handicapped and your parents have not made any special financial arrangements for that person? You may see that all of these topics need to be addressed but you may have no way of knowing whether adequate planning has been completed unless you ask your parents.

You may feel some responsibility toward your siblings to make sure that things are in order, not to mention toward your parents whose retirement and golden years may be directly affected by lack of planning. You may also feel that your parents' legal affairs will affect yours in the future if your parents do not put their affairs in order. If you, a child of the individuals directly involved, do not have the status as someone who is allowed to bring up a constructive discussion with your parents about their estates, then who does? If you do not bring it up, who will?

One of the factors that causes individuals to hesitate to bring up estate planning or incapacity planning is that they find it hard to accept that they now have to look after the person or people who always used to look after them. Sometimes it takes a very long time for this idea to dawn on a person who really does not want to reverse roles and become the caretaker.

We are not used to parenting our parents, but sometimes that is exactly what is required. You should do everything you can to ensure that your discomfort or disorientation with this issue does not prevent you from raising a topic that you think is important. You may be a "child" in the sense that you are the offspring of a certain person and therefore his or her child, but you are an adult.

Your parents might already have seen you change from a single person to a married person, or from a child to a parent of your own children. They have seen you mature from a schoolboy or schoolgirl into a person with a job and responsibilities. They might have seen all of these stages and they realize that the impulse to protect and help them is simply part of that maturation process you have been going through. As an adult, you are expected to recognize when someone close to you begins to struggle with the tasks and challenges of everyday life and to shoulder the responsibility of helping if you can.

Sometimes talking about the role reversal with your siblings, spouse, friends, or even a counselor can help you get used to the idea that you might have to take over your parents' financial or health decision-making. You will also find information about "parenting your parents" on several websites and in magazines aimed at individuals who are caretakers for their parents.

If you are willing to bring up a difficult subject with a protective attitude and willingness to listen to others, and if you are willing to prepare in advance to ensure a good outcome, then you are the right person to bring up the topic.

# Why Don't People Plan,
# and What Can You Do about That?

No two families or people are exactly alike. Their reasons for neglecting to carry out basic estate planning are never alike either, as they can be logistical, emotional, or a combination of both. However, there are some reasons that North American families and individuals give more often than others when asked about their reluctance to plan. Generally speaking, people are aware that they need to do "something" to deal with end of life and incapacity. Messages about the importance of planning are everywhere. The problem is not lack of awareness; the problem is taking action.

In this chapter, you will read about some of the reasons commonly voiced for failing to plan for the future. Some of these may sound familiar to you through your conversations with your own family members. You may even have used one or two of them yourself. If you have heard them from family members in your efforts to motivate them to get on with their planning, reading this chapter may give you more insight into their thoughts, fears, and feelings. You will find out what you are up against when you begin to plan your family meeting.

This chapter may also give you some ideas about how to counter these reasons if your parents or other relatives use them as an excuse not to plan. If some of the reasons are new to you and you have not heard them mentioned by your family members, you might find it useful to think about whether one (or more) of them is actually the true, underlying reason for their resistance to planning. If a real impediment exists, it must be dealt with so that an estate plan may be put together. However, unless the impediment is identified and revealed to you, it will never be removed.

# 1. Not Knowing Where to Start

There is no shortage of information available about wills, powers of attorney, and health-care directives and almost every related legal topic. In any given week, you could see a magazine article about retirement planning, a television program about seniors' issues, a news story about an estate gone terribly wrong, and dozens of blogs on the Internet telling you which documents you should have. Everyone has advice for you. In fact, there is so much information available that there might actually be too much for some people. It can be tough to sort out what information is reliable and what applies to you in your situation.

Public information is often doled out in snippets such as a 500-word magazine article or a four-minute television interview. Although these brief segments are very valuable in raising awareness of a topic, they are not intended to be thorough investigations of complicated legal issues. They are only overviews. Because the possible family scenarios vary so widely and legal advice changes based on the facts, it may even seem that the information you are hearing in these snippets is contradictory to what you have already heard from other sources.

It can be very confusing and frustrating if you have an abundance of information without any guidance for applying it. You may feel that you are not sure if you need a lawyer or an accountant, or both, and if you do, where you might find the right one. You may not be sure exactly what to ask for even if you do find a lawyer. Do you need advice, and if so, what kind? Which documents do you need? Should you set up a trust? Can you do anything to reduce taxes?

It is difficult to get started on a large project of any kind when you are not sure whether your information is correct or even whether you understand the full picture. The end result for most people is that planning is postponed until they have more free time to deal with something that feels immense. Frequently the postponement turns into cancellation and it never gets finished at all. This might be the stage at which your parents find themselves right now.

To narrow down the flood of information to focus on what works for you, and to find reliable, applicable help, try some of the following tips:

- Ask someone you know (e.g., family member, friend, co-worker, neighbor, long-time banker) for names of lawyers who have helped them with wills or estates in the past.

- Always use experts as opposed to generalists when consulting professionals such as doctors, accountants, and lawyers. For example, if you are going to have a full competency evaluation done for an aging parent, it is better to find a geriatric specialist than a general practitioner.

- Go to lectures or seminars held by local lawyers, accountants, financial advisors, or banks that deal with will planning. They will give you local, up-to-date information and advice that is right for your geographic area, rather than information that may be national or even international in scope.

- If you find blogs for professionals who work in your state, province, or territory, read the blogs regularly and ask plenty of questions online.

- Always look at the location of the person writing the articles, books, or blogs to see whether the information will apply to your geographic area. Remember that the law can differ drastically from place to place.

- Decide whom, of all the people offering you advice, you like and trust. Stick with that person's information and advice and work with him or her as a team. If you accept advice from too many people at the same time, you are likely to find contradictions. The contradictions arise because professionals sell advice, and their advice will be based on their experience, their judgment, the law, and your interpretation of the facts. Whenever judgment and experience come into play, there is room for a difference of opinion on what is best to do. Contradictions will be confusing and stressful for you.

You have already begun the process of planning by reading this book. You will begin to gather your thoughts as you read, and by the time you are finished, you will have a much clearer picture of what exactly your goals are for yourself and your parents, what specific issues might complicate matters for your family, and what needs to be done.

## 2. Not Knowing What It Will Cost

Most of us have to budget for large expenses. It can be hard to make room for large, unexpected bills. Many people say they do not have wills in place and have never done proper estate planning because they believe that it will be extremely expensive. They assume that if lawyers and accountants are involved, the planning process will perhaps be so expensive as to be beyond their means.

There can be a lot of uncertainty about the cost of estate planning before things get underway. As discussed in section **1.**, it is not always clear what steps need to be taken. If you do

not know what needs to be done, you certainly cannot estimate what it might cost.

Unfortunately, the cost of not planning can far exceed the cost of planning. When people pass away without having made a will, there can be lawsuits, delays, unnecessary tax liability, and financial losses to the estate. When people lose mental capacity without having put a power of attorney or health-care directive into place, sometimes the only way to deal with pressing issues is to make an application to the court for trusteeship or guardianship. Obviously the cost of a court application is going to far exceed what it would have cost to make a document in the first place.

Keep in mind that the emotional cost (of the turmoil and fighting over an estate) can mount even faster than the financial bills. It is very common for families to fight over estates and that is because estate arguments are about more than money; they are about emotional issues as well. If you fail to plan ahead, you are more than likely condemning your own family to a turbulent situation. It is worthwhile to at least find out the real cost of estate planning and not rely on guesses.

Using this book will help you keep costs down. First of all, it will give you quite a bit of information and background about estate planning and help you decide what exactly you should be doing. At the very least, you will be able to check off items that are already taken care of and then pinpoint those that still need attention. That will help you focus your requests, if any, to lawyers and accountants and save you the cost of spending hours with those advisors. If your lawyer or accountant does not have to spend time educating you about estate law in general, you will be able to use your meeting to zero in only on the issues that pertain to you.

This book will also help you hold a successful family meeting to talk about estate planning. That alone could save you thousands of dollars in fees for mediators or lawyers.

The following are some other practical ideas about maintaining control over costs when dealing with an estate-planning lawyer:

- Ask for a written quote before any work is done. Once you have that, make sure you understand what would cause the lawyer to exceed the quote.

- Understand how you are being billed. It is alright, in fact it is advisable, to ask questions about your costs before the work is done. For example, are you being charged by the hour or for the completed project? If it is for a completed project, make sure you understand exactly what is included. For example, does "estate planning" mean only wills, or are powers of attorney and health-care directives included in the price? Ask whether anybody else, such as paralegals or junior lawyers, will work on your file and what their billable hourly rate is. Also know what taxes will be added.

- Ask whether *disbursements* are extra and if so, how much they are likely to be for your file. Disbursements are out-of-pocket expenses paid by the law office, such as postage or courier fees. There might also be a set charge for faxes and photocopying.

- Ask if there is any legwork you can do yourself. For example, if the lawyer is going to search the titles to properties, you could offer to get them yourself rather than pay the lawyer to do it.

- If the lawyer calls, writes, or emails you to ask for information or documentation, or you promise to do something,

respond as promptly as you can. If you delay to the point that the lawyer has to chase you down, this is likely going to cost extra.

- Understand that requesting rewrites of documents (as opposed to asking that an error made by the lawyer, such as a misspelled name, be corrected) will probably cost extra. The lawyer's quote given at the beginning of the project is based on the average time it takes to do a project like yours, and if you keep changing your instructions so that the project changes two or three times, you will end up paying more than you were originally quoted.

- If paying a large bill all at once is a problem, ask about payment arrangements. Most law firms take credit cards. You may also be able to pay half your costs up front and the second half upon completion, or set up a payment schedule. Not all firms do this because it is risky for them, but some do, so it cannot hurt to ask.

- Keep face-to-face meetings brief and to the point. One way you can achieve this is to prepare as much as possible ahead of time. If you phone a lawyer to make your first appointment, ask what you should bring to the meeting. Make photocopies to give to the lawyer. Make notes or lists of questions to bring with you to the meeting.

## 3. Believing That Estate Planning Is Only for Rich People

The word "estate" tends to make people think of enormous homes with fenced acreages and overseas bank accounts belonging to multi-millionaires. The phrase "estate planning" can conjure up visions of corporate empires. In other words, a lot of people think that estate planning is only for the very wealthy. This is not the case. Everyone has an estate, however modest it might be. Legally, the word "estate" simply refers to what you own and what you owe, even if your net worth is in the red. Estate planning refers to deciding what you want to do with your legal and financial affairs while you are alive and after your death. It is simply not true that estate planning is only for rich people.

Estate planning is for everyone. It is important for you to deal with whatever you have accumulated during your lifetime, regardless of whether it has a higher or lower dollar value than someone else's estate. The fact that you are not rich does not mean that your spouse or children should be stuck with legal and financial problems after you have passed away.

Money is not always at the root of estate lawsuits. Although it may seem strange, estate legal battles are not always fought over large sums of money. That does happen too, of course, but estate battles are often about personal belongings or household items which have great sentimental, as opposed to monetary, value to the deceased person's family. You do not have to be wealthy to own family photo albums, mementos, heirlooms, souvenirs, or other important sentimental items.

People will fight to keep family items that have sentimental value, as evidenced by hundreds of disputes every year. The idea that estate fights only happen to wealthy people is completely wrong. We hear more about fights of wealthy families simply because the dollar amounts are so large or the families are famous. Unfortunately, the fights happen in every economic bracket.

If a dispute of an estate cannot be resolved among the people involved, it will likely end up being decided by a judge. This means court fees; lawyer's fees; accountant's fees; and miscellaneous costs such as process servers, witnesses, and time off work. If a legal battle does erupt over a personal item, it is possible that a modest estate might be completely bankrupted by fees. A lawyer is probably going to charge the same hourly rate to wage a court battle whether the fight is over a multimillion-dollar property or a family wedding ring that is only worth a couple of thousand dollars.

Looked at in the light of possible bankruptcy of the estate, it becomes even more important for a modest estate to be protected by proper planning.

When thinking about estate planning, people also forget that legal documents reveal much more than simply who gets what from the assets. For example, your will and incapacity documents tell you who your parents have chosen to put in charge of their affairs in the roles of executor, attorney (under enduring power of attorney), and health-care representative. If you do not have that information, the end result will likely be delays and confusion. The information about who is to be given legal authority over someone else's affairs is extremely important regardless of the dollar value.

## 4. Thinking They Do Not Need to Plan, Based on Anecdotes

One of the worst things people can do for themselves and their families is to make assumptions about how the law applies to them without finding out how it really works. You cannot really blame people for feeling that they are familiar with legal matters, including wills, because they hear about them all the time. Myths, urban legends, and misconceptions about wills are everywhere. Everyone has heard a few stories in the news or anecdotes during conversations at the office watercooler about sensational estate battles.

Movies, television programs, and novels feature stories about the law, including wills. We have all seen them, as they deal with important, fascinating legal dilemmas and are often extremely entertaining. Unfortunately, these shows, which are, after all, only entertainment and not documentaries, perpetuate fictionalized ideas about how wills work. The fact that it makes a good story does not make it true.

Not everyone can tell what is true and what is widely misunderstood or fictionalized for entertainment purposes. In fact, it is almost impossible. The abundance of fictional and semi-fictional stories about wills leads too many people to wrongly conclude that they are "safe" without taking any planning steps at all.

For example, many people confidently state that they do not need wills because they are married and they believe that their spouse will automatically get everything they own after they pass away. Others believe that if they do not make a will, the loved ones left behind will "know what to do" and will "do the right thing" with the deceased person's assets. Still others want to leave certain family members $1 because they think doing so will prevent the family member from bringing a lawsuit against the estate. There are dozens of these ideas being passed from person to person.

Unfortunately, none of these are particularly good ideas in terms of using the law to protect your estate and family. Though you may have heard of a case in which it appears

that a rule or idea applied and worked a certain way, it does not mean that the same thing would happen to you in your case.

For example, look at a case where there was a question about whether child support paid by a divorced father should continue on after the divorced father's death. In that case, it turned out that the estate of the deceased father did not have to pay any support after the child turned 18 years old. That was the right decision for that case, but not necessarily for yours. You should not take it as a general rule that no divorced father's estate ever has to pay support past age 18, because quite often that is not the case. It all depends on the specific facts of each case.

To add to the confusion, laws dealing with wills vary from place to place. There is no one set of laws about wills that applies to everyone, everywhere. Also, laws change over time as governments move with the times or respond to public demand, making it even harder to know what is true at any given time.

The person who assumes that he or she knows the law in detail and knows how it applies to him or her without even looking into it through reliable sources is not doing anybody any favors. He or she will never know about the mistake in the will because the mistake will have no effect until the person dies. However, the spouse, children, or siblings left behind will certainly be forced to deal with that mistake after the person has passed away.

It is always a mistake to rely on second-hand legal advice that was tailored to someone else's specifics. This includes listening to a friend or co-worker who saw a lawyer about his or her own situation and then tells you about it later, even though his or her situation seems similar to your own.

Legal advice is very fact-specific, meaning it changes from one situation to another depending on the facts of the case. Sometimes only a tiny difference between one person's estate and another can make a difference in the legal advice given. Your situation is not identical to anyone else's. Relying on someone else's secondhand legal advice is similar to taking medicine that is prescribed for another person; it can do more harm than good.

If you see a lawyer or accountant who gives you planning advice and for any reason you do not find the advice believable or correct, you can do the same thing you would with medical advice, which is seek a second opinion.

Basing your decisions on anecdotes, or stories about what happened to one particular individual, is always questionable. Making legal decisions this way can be downright dangerous. For every story you may hear about an estate that went smoothly without a will, there are 50 more stories that deliver the opposite message.

## 5. Being Too Busy

The term "sandwich generation" applies to many people reading this book. The sandwich generation refers to people, usually in their 40s or 50s, who have children at home to look after as well as aging parents to look after. They are "sandwiched" between the twin responsibilities of looking after children and looking after parents. They also have jobs and homes, marriages and social lives to look after. Part of being in that position is always being busy and having too many demands on their time.

A person in this situation will often say that he or she does not have time to review current documents, find a lawyer, have a meeting with the lawyer, look at draft documents, and then see the lawyer again to sign the will.

He or she will say that there is no time to look for documents and gather statements. Sometimes people put off the planning until some undetermined future time when they believe they will be less busy, not realizing, or perhaps not caring, that with this approach, that future time will never arrive.

The trick to fitting extra activities into an already busy life is scheduling. We all manage to fit in the annual vacation, birthdays, time off for illness, dental appointments, etc., even though each of those things is not part of our regular day. If those things can be slotted in, so can estate planning. There is nothing wrong with making an appointment with a lawyer weeks in advance, as long as you have a reliable system of keeping track of appointments so that you do not forget about it.

Another idea for fitting estate planning into a busy schedule is to break down a large project into smaller, bite-size pieces to avoid the feeling of being overwhelmed. This is one of the reasons some people like to write lists before beginning a task; it helps them feel in control of the task. You just need to accomplish one small, first step in order to feel that you have made a start and that the project is not so intimidating.

Instead of thinking "I must get my estate planning done," break it down. Start with one of the following suggestions (tailored to your situation, of course):

- "I'll ask around at work to see if anyone can recommend a good wills lawyer."

- "I'll ask my friend, Rob, which lawyer did his will for him."

- "I'll get my old will out of the safe deposit box, dust it off, and read it to remind myself of what I did last time."

- "I'll collect all of my bank statements, investment statements, and the deed to my house so that I know which assets I'm dealing with."

- "I'll make a list of my spouse and children's full names and birth dates to get ready for an appointment with the lawyer."

- "I'll read my shareholders' agreement for my business to see what it says about my share of the business on my passing away."

- "I'll call the lawyer and make an appointment."

It is probably a good idea to write down the steps you plan to take in a list so that you can check off each one as you do it.

If you are a busy person, understand that you might not get your estate planning done in as brief a time as someone else might. That is a fact of your life, and is perfectly acceptable as long as the process is begun and eventually finished. Allow yourself reasonable time so that you do not feel pressured.

## 6. Not Wanting to Give up Control

The question of giving up control shows up more in incapacity planning than it does in will planning, though people do worry about it in both situations. Most parents are startled or dismayed at even hearing the words that their son or daughter is prepared to take control of the family home, business, cottage, banking, or investments. Nobody likes to feel as if they are being pushed aside, particularly when it is their own money and future that are being discussed.

You should realize that one of the biggest stressors for parents is the fear that once the documents are in place, the children will simply do whatever they want, without consulting the parents or following the parents' financial values. Whether or not this is a realistic fear is irrelevant to how parents might feel.

For example, many parents feel that they have spent a lifetime saving money and investing conservatively to help their nest egg grow. They feel that they have done alright for themselves doing things a certain, usually conservative, way. They worry that should the children be put in charge, the children might invest speculatively or foolishly or spend frivolously, thereby wasting all those years of saving and investing. This fear can exist even when there is no factual basis or past incident by the children to support it.

There are ways to put these fears to rest, or at least to reduce them, and some ideas to combat those fears include:

- Not all incapacity documents put the children in charge as soon as the document is signed. In fact, the vast majority of documents do not. An enduring power of attorney is specifically designed to be used as a planning ahead tool. (For alternate names for an enduring power of attorney, see the Introduction.) The enduring power of attorney document is signed by a parent while he or she has mental capacity and it legally "endures" or "continues" once the parent loses capacity. With this type of document, the children cannot exercise any legal authority over a parent's assets until the parent has been declared incompetent. The declaration is usually provided by a doctor or by two doctors. Knowing that he or she will still have control of assets and finances after the documents are signed will probably go a long way toward dealing with a parent's anxiety on that point.

- Whether the document that is signed is used immediately, or is designed to be used in the future, is up to your parents and depends on what help they need. Your parents retain control of the document and of their financial affairs as long as they have mental capacity.

- In most jurisdictions, the parent can include specific controls or requirements for accountability that would come into effect once the children start using the enduring power of attorney. This kind of clause is not included very often in enduring powers of attorney, but that is largely because people are not aware of them and do not realize that they can request them. The popularity of this sort of clause is slowly catching on. For example, an enduring power of attorney might require the children to give a full accounting of everything they have done with the parent's finances to someone else on a regular basis; for example, once a year. The person that they must give the accounting to might be the parent's lawyer or accountant, but it is much more frequently another family member. For example, if you were to be appointed as the representative under the enduring power of attorney, you might have to give an accounting to one of your siblings once a year.

- Providing this kind of accounting prevents a representative from operating in secrecy. It often acts as a deterrent against someone who is tempted to do something with the parent's money that he or she knows ought not to be done. The possibility of being found out usually deters people.

- Another alternative is that the document might specifically say that family members have a right to demand an accounting whenever they want one. The purpose is to bring transparency to what the children are doing, in the hopes that will keep the children honest as well as reduce the number of questions and disputes that might arise. These are just examples, as documents are always tailored to the specific situation of the parent and his or her family, but they show how it is possible to make sure that the children in charge do not simply operate in secrecy.

- Try to find a lawyer who specializes in estate planning so that your parent knows that he or she is getting experienced advice from someone who knows all of the ins and outs of incapacity. Do not allow an accountant, a banker, an investment advisor, or a law student to draft the documents. Understand that the real value in the estate-planning process is not necessarily the piece of paper itself but the discussion, ideas, and advice that take place while the documents are being planned. Your parents should maximize that part of the process so that they have a chance to ask questions and explore options. There is simply no replacement for the peace of mind your parents will gain by talking with someone who really knows how wills and incapacity documents work and can anticipate problems before they have a chance to occur.

- Stay out of the meeting that takes place between your parent and the lawyer.

Even when your parent feels that he or she wants the moral support of you being there, you should try to avoid being in the room. If it cannot be avoided that you are there, stay quiet and let your parent do the talking. If you are the one asking and answering the questions, you are the one getting the legal advice and not your parent. Also, the fact that your parent cannot speak for himself or herself may mean that capacity is already diminished, and hiding this fact from the lawyer is only going to result in the wrong documents being prepared. The lawyer may even refuse to prepare documents for your parent unless the lawyer is able to meet alone with the parent for at least part of the meeting. This should be comforting to your parent in that it shows that the lawyer is interested in helping the parent achieve his or her goals only.

## 7. Not Knowing How to Hold a Family Meeting

Plenty of people might like the idea of getting together with everyone and having a meeting, but most families are not in the habit of holding formal meetings. In fact a family meeting, particularly a formal one with note-taking and a chairperson, would be rare to nonexistent for the majority of families. Most of us would not know how to go about it, how to gain the cooperation of others, or what to do afterward to make everything legally effective.

In other families, there are topics that are not only left unmentioned, they are purposely avoided. In some families, subjects such as family finance or planning how to deal with the death of a parent are taboo. The parents simply do not wish to discuss financial or personal affairs with their children under any circumstances. These are the hardest families in which to hold a meeting because the culture of the family works strongly against the success of such a meeting. Generally emotions will run the highest in this type of family, making rational conversations about legal topics very hard to hold.

This does not mean it cannot be done. It means that extra care must be taken to preserve the privacy and dignity of the parents so that they are comfortable. It also means that the children in this kind of family must have time and encouragement to adjust to their new roles in the family.

Reading this book will give you both an overview to help you set realistic expectations for a family meeting, and detailed information on holding the meeting itself. On the CD that accompanies this book you will find a Family Meeting Checklist and other useful forms to help you organize and conduct your meeting. Consider sharing the parts of this book that you find most helpful with your family members.

## 8. There Is No Consensus on What to Do

This is not a reason to put off having a meeting. In fact, it is one of the best reasons in favor of having a meeting. One of the main goals of holding family meetings is to get to a consensus on important issues. It likely will not happen instantly. You should anticipate that it may take more than one meeting to make decisions, if people are starting with no preconceived ideas. Your first discussion will probably be a general one about the need to do some planning and to pinpoint the areas that need to be covered. After that you will set out some time lines and goals to be achieved and go from there.

If your family's estate-planning needs are complex, realize that you may end up having several meetings, each of which builds on what was done or decided in the meeting before. This is not at all unusual. Estate planning is always a process and you should not be dismayed or discouraged by the fact that it will not be accomplished in one day.

You should understand that your family may never reach the point where everyone agrees about what should be done about your parents' estates. Is the consensus of everyone on every issue actually necessary? Your parents might have plans that some of the children will agree with and others will not, but as it is your parents' estates it is their right to make that decision. Perhaps the purpose of your family meetings is not to get everyone's agreement but simply to let everyone know what your parents are planning to do. Perhaps everyone will have to agree to disagree.

## 9. Privacy Concerns

Anyone undergoing the process of estate planning will have to divulge detailed information about his or her income, assets, and debts to the estate-planning lawyer. That is the only way a client is going to get accurate advice about what to do. Estate planning is like a jigsaw puzzle in which all the pieces (i.e., family, business, money, health, retirement) have to fit together, and they only fit if all of the pieces are revealed. The person who wants to do estate planning may also have to discuss these topics with an accountant or a financial advisor in order to get appropriate advice.

Many parents say that they do not want their children involved in the estate-planning process because they do not want to reveal confidential information to anyone other than their professional advisors. They believe their financial affairs are none of the children's business,

and it is their right to maintain that. Because of this wish for privacy, many parents put off their estate planning, believing that they must tell their children about everything they own.

This concern for privacy should not prevent your parents from going ahead with their planning. The extent of your involvement or that of your siblings or other family members can be controlled according to your parents' wishes. It is everyone's right to keep their financial and personal matters private if they so choose. Some parents choose to tell their children about their finances and others do not. It is very much a personal decision so you should do your best to work with it.

If your involvement in their planning goes no further than motivating them to get started, and perhaps helping them find a lawyer, you can probably alleviate most of their concerns about privacy. If they do not tell you themselves about what they own and the value of their holdings, there is no way for you to know about these things.

A compromise might be that your parents will tell you about the kind of assets they have, and possibly where the assets are located (e.g., where they bank and where title deeds are stored) without having to tell you the dollar amounts. This will allow them some amount of privacy while still allowing you and any professional advisors to understand the situation.

For example, you can understand whether the family home is owned by both parents or by only one without knowing the appraised value of it. You can know whether there is life insurance without knowing the dollar amount. You can know whether they still own shares in a business they retired from years ago without knowing the share value. In this way, you can preserve their privacy while getting going on the planning.

Even if you share the same lawyer with your parents, the lawyer is bound by solicitor-client confidentiality, which is the duty of every lawyer to keep each client's legal affairs confidential. This can become extremely important in smaller towns where there are not many lawyers and whole families consult one lawyer about various matters. You can assure your parents that the lawyer will not share a client's information with anyone, including family members, without specific permission from them to do so.

People also sometimes feel that during the estate-planning process, they are being pressured into revealing financial details that they would otherwise prefer to keep private. Many older people just do not like letting the world in general know how much they have put away and it makes them uncomfortable and resentful if they are pressured for that information. They should not have to reveal information they do not want to reveal to family members.

Understand that estate planning can be done without your parent having to divulge details about the amounts held in bank accounts or investments. The *type* of asset and the way it is held (e.g., joint owners, sole owner) are much more important in the planning process than the actual dollar amount. If your parent is concerned about giving out too much financial information, suggest to him or her that he or she divulge that information only to the lawyer, who is not allowed to tell other people.

## 10.  Superstition

A surprisingly large number of people fear that if they write a will, they are somehow fatally jinxing themselves. They fear that the act of signing that piece of paper that talks about their death will in some inexplicable way cause their death to occur. If this were actually the case, a large fraction of our society would pass away every day, as wills are signed all over the world.

Superstitions can be hard to overcome simply because they are not really grounded in any real experience or fact, and therefore cannot really be countered with logic. A person with this kind of superstition is really suffering from an exaggeration of everyone's natural fear of dying.

Just as opening a bank account will not cause you to win the lottery or saying hello to the dentist will not make your teeth fall out, there is no causal link between making a will and passing away. Everyone in the world dies eventually, with or without a will.

3

# What Are the Consequences of Not Planning?

Having looked at the reasons why many individuals and families do not do any estate planning, we should now look at what they get out of completing their estate planning. Many people acknowledge that having a will would be a good idea but really do not fully understand what a will, an enduring power of attorney, and a health-care directive can really do for them when properly prepared. The documents do much more than most people realize. After reading this chapter, you should have a much greater understanding of the consequences of not having these documents in place.

The main purposes of a will, an enduring power of attorney, and a health-care directive are to express your wishes for you when you are no longer able to do so. They might cover anything from who would raise your minor children after your death to who will choose which long-term care facility you live in to who will receive your assets. These are truly important matters to each and every one of us and should not be left to interpretation, guesswork, or debate.

In terms of talking to your family about estate planning, it is a good idea for you to know the downside of lack of planning as well, so that you can motivate others to stay on track and to complete the planning once it has been started. As you read through the following sections, you will no doubt find yourself thinking, "That could easily happen in my family." All of the situations discussed in this book are based on the experiences of thousands of families who have neglected to do their planning. Every family is different but you will be able to identify the scenarios that are most likely to occur in your own situation.

# 1. Lawsuits

You should expect that if you do no estate planning at all, there will likely be arguments among family members. That is so common as to be almost universal. The arguments could be about what funeral arrangements should be made, who is to be in charge of your estate, who is to get which assets, or whether a promise you made to someone years ago is to be honored. In fact, there is absolutely no limit to the possibilities for disputes on estates, as the subject matter can be financial or personal, or both. Although not every dispute becomes a lawsuit, unfortunately many do.

One of the reasons that arguments flare up into lawsuits on estates more than they might otherwise is that people's emotions are close to the surface. After the family has lost a loved one, they generally do not react and speak as rationally as they would have done before the death. Emotions creep into the discussion, as people are grieving. Whereas they could have sat around the dinner table talking calmly about matters a week before, now they are upset.

During a dispute on an estate, people will bring in emotional (as opposed to rational) arguments such as, "This is what he would have wanted." While it can be nearly impossible to know what a deceased person wanted in the absence of proper documentation, this does become one of the arguments heard most often. Even though it is generally used as if the person saying it considers it to be the final word on the matter, rather than settling disputes, it tends to aggravate them. Simply put, family members do not agree on "what he would have wanted."

Similarly, if the lawsuit is about issues relating to a parent's incapacity, you will likely find that the parent becomes a weapon in the lawsuit. One person will try to prevent another person from having any access to the parent in order to pressure the other person into agreeing on something. Both sides will try to get the parent to say something negative about the other person. Although this does not advance either side of the lawsuit and only makes things immeasurably miserable for the parent, it is not at all unusual. People behave badly in this situation. The justification given, whether supported by the facts or not, is always that one person is doing what he or she thinks is best for the parent, while those on the other side will believe that exactly the opposite approach would be good for the parent.

A lawsuit on an estate of an incapacitated adult is always bad news for the parent in question as well as for the rest of the family. A lawsuit will cause delays, expenses, and injured feelings. As with any kind of lawsuit, there is never any certainty as to what a judge will decide at the end of a trial or hearing. This means that there is also a lot of speculation and worry during the course of the lawsuit.

Quite often, the costs of a lawsuit on an estate are paid at least in part by the estate itself. This means that the individuals battling each other, or at least some of them, do not have to pay the lawyers and other expenses up front themselves. This can have the effect of making a person more likely to stubbornly carry on the lawsuit longer than he or she would have done had he or she had to pay for it out of his or her own money.

Unfortunately not only does that prolong a bitter estate fight, it uses up the assets of the estate so that the losers are the individual beneficiaries who would have inherited the money had it not been spent on fighting.

## 2. Damaged Family Relationships

Most people who have had the misfortune of being part of a disputed estate will agree that the worst damage done in the course of the dispute was to family relationships. Money and property are often lost as well, but their loss is rarely felt as deeply as that of the estrangement of a relative. An estate in dispute often causes siblings and spouses to argue, sometimes irrevocably, even when those individuals used to get along.

Disputes can, and do, break out over anything from funeral arrangements to cash payouts, and anything in between. Even in families who usually interact and communicate well, the emotional strain of losing a beloved family member can interfere with normal interactions. Emotions often run high and close to the surface and are triggered more easily than usual. People are not at their best. People say things in the heat of the moment that cannot be taken back.

When family members fight over visitation to their parents or who gets to keep family heirlooms, it can be impossible for them to reconcile once the fight is over, due to the emotional content of the battle. Many families never recover from the effects of an estate lawsuit. Individuals should do everything they can to avoid putting their loved ones through this.

Most estate disputes can be avoided if there is up-to-date, accurate, effective legal documentation in place that is tailored to the needs of the specific person. Another way to avoid disputes is to talk out matters in a family meeting so that nobody is surprised at what is in the will, and nobody accuses his or her siblings of pressuring the parents into doing something they did not really want to do. The child who is disappointed by what his or her parents are planning to put into the will might still be disappointed, but at least he or she will not blame it on siblings and begin a lawsuit.

## 3. Delays in the Administration of an Estate

When there is a lawsuit on an estate, the entire estate has to wait until the dispute is resolved either by the parties themselves or by the court. The money in the estate cannot be distributed to the beneficiaries because the judge might order that the will be overturned and a different distribution is to take place.

This can mean that beneficiaries do not receive their inheritances for years. This is generally not beneficial to anyone. The delay could mean that beneficiaries receive less than they would have otherwise, as property values decline, companies go out of business, or the estate is invested at a poor rate of return. Or it could simply be the case that the estate is slowly drained by legal fees, accounting fees, property taxes, maintenance for real estate holdings, investment and banking fees, and other expenses that add up.

Even when there is not a lawsuit going on, there can be major delays for other reasons. Nobody wants delays on estates, not just because of loss of money, which is certainly annoying enough in itself, but because people want to put the death of a loved one behind them and move on. They want to feel a sense of closure for emotional reasons.

Sometimes a delay is caused because the person who died left a homemade or handwritten will. The chance of running into delays with homemade wills is many times that of delays with professionally prepared wills. There is expertise required to draft a strong will that deflects problems, and most people do not have that expertise any more than they have the expertise to remove their own appendix or fill their own dental cavities. In other words, it can be done, but success is more a matter of luck than anything else in that case.

Many handwritten wills contain errors or deficiencies that the person who wrote the will simply did not intend. This is partly because some words in law have meanings other than what we usually attribute to them in non-law situations. For example, the word "children" can be a problem. A man making a will who says "I leave my estate to my children" is almost always intending that the estate will go to the children of his marriage.

What he generally does not consider is whether "my children" includes the child he had out of wedlock when he was a teenager and who has never been a part of his life. He also does not usually clarify whether he means to include his wife's children from her previous marriage, that is, his stepchildren, particularly since in most cases stepchildren are not legally adopted. Often the law does not say what we think it will say.

Typically, homemade wills mention assets that are not properly described, such as referring to "my necklace" when in fact the person owned several necklaces. There is a delay while appraisals are done and the executor figures out how to give a necklace that will please both the beneficiary of the necklace and the other beneficiaries of the estate.

There can also be confusion over which beneficiary he or she actually intended to include because the person is described only by a first name or nickname, or the writing is impossible to read. When a will mentions, for example, that the tools in the garage are to go to "Dan," and the deceased person had both a son named "Daniel" and a grandson called "Danny," there is a delay while the executor deals with the confusion.

Sometimes, impossible conditions are placed on gifts. For example, a clause in a will that says, "My son will inherit one half of my estate as long as he does not marry his girlfriend, Jane" would not be valid, but many people include that kind of thing without realizing it has no validity. Again, there is a delay while the executor deals with the legal fallout of the mistake in the will.

When this kind of mistake happens, and they do often happen to well-intentioned but unsuspecting individuals, the unclear parts of the will have to be sorted out before the estate can be settled. The executor is not going to simply choose any interpretation at random, as no matter what he or she chooses, someone will be unhappy and will challenge him or her. This will expose the executor to legal liability.

Sometimes certain discrepancies or confusion can be settled by way of agreement of all beneficiaries, but most often it will require a formal interpretation by the courts. Even an agreement among beneficiaries often needs to be negotiated or mediated by lawyers. So once the discrepancy or mistake exists in the will, it takes time and money to figure it out.

People think of a will as a means of distributing assets, which of course it is, but it does more than that. One of the main purposes of a will is to put someone in charge of the estate by naming him or her as the executor. If there is a will, the executor can start looking after the estate immediately without a court order or any other official approval. However, if there is no will, nobody can act on behalf of the estate without being appointed by the court. Obviously it will take at least a few weeks, if not longer, to get a court order appointing someone.

Think about all of the things that an executor would normally do for an estate in the first few weeks:

- Make funeral arrangements.

- Notify family members of their inheritance.

- Put a notice in the paper.

- Notify banks and insurance companies.

- Hire a lawyer to probate the will.

- Make sure that all assets such as the items in the deceased's home are secure.

Now imagine the chaos that can erupt when there is no executor to take care of those tasks. If nobody is in charge for the first few weeks after a person passes away, there is nobody legally able to do most of those tasks and there may be confusion and financial losses in addition to the delay.

A part of wills that is unfamiliar to non-lawyers, and as a result usually gets completely left out of homemade wills is the section that contains clauses that are generally known as "powers" or "authorities." This is the part of the will that enables the executor to legally do what the will has asked him or her to do by giving specific legal powers to the executor.

For example, every year an executor must prepare a tax return for an estate. The executor is legally obligated by the very fact that he or she is an executor to try to save as much on taxes as possible. The executor hires an accountant who advises that there are *tax elections*, which are basically choices as to which way to go, such as a loss carryback that could be used to reduce taxes.

The government might look at the will that named the person as executor and decide that the will does not actually authorize the executor to speak for the deceased person on tax matters. If that is the case, the executor will have to approach the court to ask for permission to make the tax election. This could have been avoided as most professionally prepared wills contain all the powers needed for a smooth estate administration without resorting to the courts.

A similar situation frequently arises when real estate (including homes, cottages, lake properties, and mineral rights) has to be sold from an estate. The rules about sale of real property from an estate are somewhat complicated and there are certain choices that an executor has to make to carry out the sale. Again, court permission might be required if the will itself does not convey the needed legal power to deal with the sale.

Unfortunately, all of these problems could have been avoided had the will contained the right mix of powers. When the powers are missing or inadequate, the executor has to resort to the courts, even when none of the beneficiaries of the estate are contesting his or her actions, and the court applications put everything else in the estate on hold.

## 4. Financial Loss, Fraud, or Financial Mismanagement

As part of your estate planning, you must plan for someone else to have control of your finances either after you pass away, or while you are alive but incapacitated. At some point, you have to relinquish control of them to someone else and if you do not do your planning, you lose control over what happens when you do pass that right to another person.

When you pass away, your executor will control your assets and liabilities for the purpose of transferring your estate to your beneficiaries. While you are alive but incapacitated, your attorney (under power of attorney) will control your assets and debts for you on your behalf either until you recover your capacity or you pass away.

One of the most important aspects of advance planning is that you get to choose who the person in control will be. You can name your executor and name your attorney under a power of attorney. This means that you can pick someone you trust or someone who is good with money, or both. You can think about potential weaknesses of the person you have appointed, such as a person who is honest and detail-oriented but is not good with money. Or perhaps you were going to pick someone who is good with money but is too easily influenced by others. You can then make arrangements to do something about those weaknesses.

For example, you could name more than one person to represent you, giving your executor or attorney someone to help with the financial statements, bookkeeping, and investing parts of the estate. You could choose two people who together would fulfill all of your requirements.

If you fail to plan ahead, you will lose control of the decision. You will have no say in who is appointed to represent you while you are alive (power of attorney) or after you pass away (will). The person who is appointed might not be someone you approve of, for many reasons. It might be someone who is terrible with money. It might be someone who tends to invest foolishly. It might even be someone dishonest who might use your money for his or her own purposes and not for your benefit. You can retain control of the decision and help head off this kind of financial mismanagement by choosing your representatives in advance while you are healthy.

Of course, choosing them yourself does not guarantee that everything will run smoothly. Even an honest person can mismanage finances. However, you will certainly have a better chance of success if you put some thought into who it will be rather than if you simply left it to chance.

Beyond the choice of who is in control, there is the issue of how the person can be regulated. Properly made wills and powers of attorney can contain restrictions on what a representative can do, and can also contain guidelines to follow. The documents in most jurisdictions allow for more flexibility than is usually used.

For example, you could state in your enduring power of attorney that you want your representative to invest your money in a very conservative way. You could direct your attorney not to sell your lakeside cottage because you plan to give it to someone in your will. You could state how much people are to be paid to represent you. By setting out these clear guidelines, you make it easy for the person to understand what to do, and easy for anybody else, such as family members, to spot financial problems before they get too big to reverse.

You might also consider including a clause in your enduring power of attorney that would require your attorney to give a full financial accounting to a person of your choice at predetermined intervals. An accounting is a summary of all the money or property the attorney received on your behalf, a summary of all expenses, and an up-to-date balance of monies held. For example, you could say that your attorney must give an accounting to your lawyer, brother, wife, or friend every year.

Knowing that someone else is going to see the financial statement will usually deter a person from stealing from you or borrowing money that is almost certainly never going to be paid back. Even if the person does steal from you, the problem is going to be spotted and resolved much more quickly if the statements are distributed to a third person. Otherwise, fraud or theft could go on for years with nobody knowing about it, by which time you might have nothing left to steal.

## 5. Family Business May Be Damaged or Destroyed

The successful transfer of a family business or small business to the next generation or to a third party takes months, if not years, of planning. As a business owner, you have to choose a new owner (called a *successor*), who could be one of your children, another member of your family, a group of managers or employees, or an independent person (usually a purchaser).

Once the successor has been chosen, unless you are selling outright to a stranger, he or she has to be groomed by you to take over one day. This is usually done by a combination of formal education, hands-on training, and on-the-job experience, all of which is driven by you and the successor working together. At the same time, other family members are informed as to the eventual ownership of the business so that each of them will know the role he or she is to play. For example, the other family members will know whether they will be shareholders, directors, employees, or not involved in any way.

If you have not done any planning, you run the risk that your children will argue over which of them is to be the next owner of the business. If you have a spouse, nieces, nephews, sons-in-law, daughters-in-law, or other family members involved in the business, they will take sides.

There is also the possibility that you want to sell the business to a group of employees by way of a management buyout, or that you want to sell the business outright to an independent purchaser. If you have not done any planning and have not documented your plans and wishes on paper, you will have no reason to assume that your plans will be carried out if you lose capacity or pass away.

If you should lose capacity without having an enduring power of attorney in place that appoints someone to act as your representative, your business will likely suffer. Particularly in small businesses, the signature of the owner is usually required for payroll, lease renewals, taking on major contracts, making large purchases such as equipment, and paying suppliers. You are probably the only person who can file documents at the company registry and sign shareholders' resolutions to run the company. Think about how long your business could survive with that kind of uncertainty and delay.

If you pass away without having made provision for your business in your will, there will likely be enormous delays while your family members search for documentation, argue among themselves, and eventually reach a conclusion about who is to own the business. There is absolutely no guarantee that the decisions they make will be anything like the ones you would have made. If you want to have some control about the future of your business, you have to do your own succession planning.

In Canada, see *Succession Planning Kit for Canadian Business*, also published by Self-Counsel Press.

## 6. Paying Too Much Tax

Taxation is always an issue when someone passes away. The United States has inheritance taxes. Canada does not, but both countries have capital gains tax. Other taxes come into play as well, such as taxes that have been deferred when income is placed in registered retirement accounts, or income tax returns that the deceased person never filed for some reason. In both countries, planning ahead of time can save an individual or family many thousands of dollars.

Doing estate planning in advance while everyone is healthy and the lines of communication are open gives you opportunities to explore options. For example, you may want to look at different trust arrangements for children or families that will save thousands of dollars in tax, but will only work if they are actually put into place either before you pass away, or they are put into your will.

Planning in advance also gives you the chance to look at possible arrangements for passing your business or vacation property to your children or grandchildren. If you own real estate other than your own principal residence when you pass away, you are likely to incur a large tax bill for the transfer of that property, even if it is held in joint names. By planning ahead, you and your accountant should be able to figure out the most tax-effective way of holding those titles.

If it looks like there is no way to reduce the tax hit beyond the preparation you have already done, you may be able to purchase a life insurance policy payable to your estate that would provide cash flow to pay those taxes. This would mean that your family could still keep the properties and not have to sell them to pay taxes.

## 7. Likelihood That More Intrusive Help Will Be Needed Later

This section applies more to failing to plan for incapacity than it does to failing to plan for passing away. It is important to realize that refusing to talk about or think about your future physical and mental health will not help matters. Nobody knows in advance whether they will suffer from an injury or health issue that causes them to lose mental capacity, so it is a good idea to have a plan in place in case it happens.

By putting a health-care directive and an enduring power of attorney in place, you have made it much less likely that anyone will ever

have to apply to the courts to be appointed as your guardian and/or trustee. Keep in mind that creating documents ahead of time for a few hundred dollars is much easier and less expensive than having someone go through a court process at your expense. More importantly, by having these documents in place you can control and restrict the amount of power the person has over you. Instead of having a court-appointed person who has control of absolutely every aspect of your health care with no input from you, you could have a health-care directive that chooses who will represent you, puts some limits on the decisions that can be made, and gives some guidance about your wishes.

You could, for example, use a health-care directive to talk about how you feel about "pulling the plug" when there is no hope of recovery no matter what is done. You can talk about whether or not you would like to donate tissues and organs for transplant after you pass away. If you do not make and document these decisions for yourself, you run the risk of someone being appointed by the court to make them for you, or of family members arguing among themselves about what to do.

## 8. More Emotional Upheaval

There is no question that the death of a loved one is one of life's most stressful and upsetting events. Realizing that a beloved family member has lost his or her mental capacity is not far behind in terms of the emotional upset it causes. All of this is bad enough, but is made so much harder when the surviving family members do not know what the person wanted done in that situation.

For example, making funeral arrangements for one of your parents is not a pleasant or happy job. However, consider how much more disagreeable it would be if you had to fight with your siblings about whether there should be burial or cremation, open casket or private memorial, or a religious or nonreligious service.

These matters are of utmost emotional importance to the surviving family members and almost everyone will have an opinion about what the deceased person wanted done for a funeral. Everyone will be adamant that his or her opinion is correct, based on his or her relationship with the person who has passed away. People will dig in their heels and insist on certain arrangements, much more than they would on matters that did not have so much emotional impact. The arguing and the resulting tears or screaming matches will make everything so much harder for everyone.

Think about how much easier it would be on everyone if the deceased person had simply left a written note that outlined his or her wishes about funeral, burial, or cremation. Not everyone will like the choice but most will not argue if they are sure it is what the deceased person really wanted.

A similar thing happens when a parent loses capacity. All of a sudden everyone knows what is best for the incapacitated person and arguments break out about what should be done, who should do it, and who should pay for it. In a way, this upheaval can be worse than the upset when someone passes away simply because the incapacity could go on for many years. Small disputes grow into larger ones over time and eventually the children are fighting about who gets to visit the incapacitated parent, who decides what treatment is best, and whether the house should be sold. Much of the arguing and injured feelings could have been spared by some advance planning by the parent.

# 9. Fewer Options as Capacity Diminishes

Signing estate-planning documents and incapacity planning documents requires mental capacity, or the ability to make reasonable decisions for yourself. For this reason, estate planning is best done early while people are mentally healthy. Realistically, however, not everybody is ready or motivated to take care of their planning early and do not take steps until they have no choice because they are beginning to lose mental or physical health. There is no question that many people do not do anything about estate planning or incapacity planning until they are shocked into doing so by a health scare or the realization that they are showing the first signs of memory loss.

As the early, small signs of mental incapacity evolve into more frequent and more pronounced periods of memory loss or confusion, options for planning are decreased. Each advancement of incapacity reduces options and makes things more complicated, time consuming, and costly.

For example, if a will is signed while a person is completely healthy mentally, there is no need for back-up of the document by third parties. If, however, the will is signed during the period of time in which incapacity is in the early stages, it may need to be supported by an assessment by a doctor indicating that the person really did understand that he or she was signing a will.

If you leave it so late that capacity is greatly diminished or no longer present at all, it is too late to make a will. At that point the person will lose control over the process, can no longer sign documents, and will have the administration of his or her estate controlled by the courts. That of course involves lawyers, doctors, and accountants. As you can see, each step takes longer, is more costly, and takes more autonomy away from the person whose estate it is.

Some specific situations are better resolved and have more options if they are planned well in advance. For example, a business owner who plans ahead to sell his or her business, prepares his or her financial statements, and fixes up his or her business for sale will have the time to consider several offers before accepting the one that suits him or her best. If no planning has been done and the business has to be sold, as is, in a hurry, the owner is probably going to end up selling at a fire-sale price that is much lower than he or she could have attained with more time to prepare.

## 10. Are Some Situations More Urgent Than Others?

While it is important that everyone put an estate plan into place, it is not urgent for most people that it be completed immediately. For most people, it is alright if it takes a month or two before the planning is completed. It is possible to agree that something is important without agreeing that it is urgent. For some people though, their planning is both important and urgent — we will look at some of these situations in this section.

As you read in the previous section, the onset of dementia or incapacity causes an individual's estate planning to become urgent because time is running out. However, even where capacity is not an issue at all, there can be circumstances which make it vital that the individual take some steps immediately to get things in order.

Planning will be more urgent if the person's situation is time sensitive. If someone has had a heart attack and is not recovering well, or is suffering with terminal cancer, he or she will soon lose the opportunity to do any planning if he or she delays taking action. As terminal diseases progress, sometimes pain medication is increased and unfortunately that interferes with mental capacity, again diminishing the time available for the signing of documents.

Urgency can also arise from the circumstances of an elderly person's life that make his or her situation more complicated. When there are complications, the potential for lawsuits is much greater than when things are simpler and therefore it is more urgent that proper planning be done.

For example, an aging person might own a business but has not made it clear which of his or her children will own the business one day (known as the aging person's *successor*), or whether the business is to be sold outside the family. If there is more than one child interested in having the business, costly legal disputes and family conflicts could arise. Also, business planning should be done over a matter of years to allow for the proper selection of a successor, the effective training of the successor to run the business, and the arrangement of legal and accounting matters to minimize taxes that will have to be paid when the business is transferred.

Another situation in which planning becomes urgent arises when an aging person has been married more than once or has had more than one common-law relationship. The situation is even more complicated when there are children from more than one relationship. The aging person needs to choose someone to represent him or her as an executor under a will and as an attorney under a power of attorney. He or she also needs to state who is to get what from the estate once he or she passes away.

Few blended families, no matter how well they get along under normal circumstances, are able to resolve all of these issues amicably if the aging person simply has not put any plans in place. This is not necessarily because family members are greedy or interfering; it is usually the case that both "families" legitimately feel that they would be the best representative.

Planning also becomes urgent when an aging person's family is geographically distant. These days, people often move long distances to find work or to maximize family opportunities. It is not unusual for an aging person to have no children or siblings nearby. An aging person in this situation needs to give serious thought to who would be willing and available to help if he or she began to lose mental capacity. Also, the children and other family members need to be told who has been chosen to fill various roles so that they will know how to respond in case of an emergency.

# Talking to
# Your Parents

One of the most commonly asked questions, and one of the hardest to answer, is how to start a difficult conversation with your parents. How do you tell a parent that you believe he or she is losing mental capacity and that he or she has to take legal steps to deal with it? How do you motivate reluctant or uninterested parents (or other relatives) to take care of their planning? Nobody really wants to talk about it, so how does the conversation ever get started? Just as importantly, once it is started, how do you make sure that it ends up being channeled into a viable plan for the family to act upon?

The expectation that this conversation is going to be difficult is almost universal. If we accept that the conversation will not be easy and we understand the reasons behind the difficulty, perhaps we can learn to overcome the issues. This chapter will talk about how to hold a difficult conversation with your parents (as opposed to a meeting with all family members present) in a way that is less stressful, more empathetic, and more productive.

Always keep in mind that the end result of the conversation should be a legally binding and effective plan for the future. It is not enough to have the conversation and then just walk away from what you have heard. Because this is the goal, you will find that your discussions with your parents have to be thorough even when you feel as if you really do not want to talk about it anymore, and you eventually have to convince them to make some decisions.

## 1. Make the Subject Less Negative

Some topics have unwritten values attached to them that we react to without consciously realizing it. For example, some life events are generally agreed upon as good news for those who are involved, such as weddings, promotions at work, or winning the lottery. Other life events are generally agreed upon as bad news, such as divorces and bankruptcies.

Unfortunately, almost all aspects of estate planning fall within the "bad news" category. It is almost impossible to characterize life events such as dying or becoming critically ill as anything else. Without even having to consciously understand or articulate the reasons, we know that talking about estate planning will involve talking about unpleasant subjects. This is the challenge you are facing.

Everyone agrees that it is hard to bring up a sensitive topic such as asking your parents to plan for their eventual passing away. It is even tougher to bring up planning for mental incapacity. In most families, talking about money is also taboo. Many people who fully understand the need for planning to be done still delay doing anything about it because they simply do not want to open up emotional or controversial subjects with family members.

If you are uncomfortable talking about death, particularly with beloved family members, you are certainly not alone. Avoidance is a very natural reaction to unpleasant topics. This is why in most conversations about estate planning you will not usually hear an individual say "when I die"; instead you will hear the person say "when I pass away," "when my time is up," "when I'm gone," "when I kick the bucket," or most commonly, "when something happens to me."

Our society has several euphemisms for dying, and for good reason. You do not want to frighten, sadden, or upset your listener, but you strongly suspect you will do so when you bring up certain topics. Euphemisms help to keep a little bit of distance between yourself and the idea of dying. This is certainly understandable; nobody wants to be the cause of tears or sleepless nights. If a family member is terminally ill, or shows signs of dementia, the task of bringing up estate planning seems impossible. Take comfort in the fact that almost everyone feels the same way.

Added to the discomfort of the topic itself is the worry about setting off sensitive family dynamics. Almost every family has at least one or two individuals who have had disputes with relatives or personalities who clash with others. Sometimes getting along with certain family members is a matter of delicate balance. If harmony has historically been hard to achieve in your family, it might seem to go against the grain to disturb it now by talking about difficult issues. In other words, it is just easier not to start a fight by bringing up a sensitive topic.

Often people think that talking about death and money in the same conversation is distasteful. They worry about looking greedy if they ask their parents if they have made a will. However, estate planning and incapacity planning are not just about money. They are also about looking after each other in the family, protecting loved ones, making provisions for minor children or grandchildren, and showing respect for the wishes of those doing the planning.

Having said all of the above about how negatively people perceive estate planning, it is possible to see estate planning and incapacity planning in a positive light, once you understand the process and its benefits. It will make your conversation with your parents much easier if you focus on the positive rather than the negative and use words that have positive connotations. You need to understand, and help your parents to understand, that thinking about planning is not the same as thinking about dying. Estate planning and incapacity planning are about the following:

- Finding ways to protect your loved ones financially.

- Sparing your family the pain of trying to figure out your wishes and possibly even fighting over them.

- Giving back to your community or cherished causes by leaving money to charities, churches, or schools.

- Making sure that your wishes are carried out either during your lifetime under a power of attorney or after you have passed away.

- Giving yourself and your family peace of mind.

- Staying in control of your own affairs as long as possible.

- Preventing costly or upsetting mistakes.

- Preserving the value of assets, property, or businesses.

- Showing other people that you will respect their stated wishes.

Perhaps you can choose two or three of the above points and use them as an opener for your conversation. No doubt you will cover many of those points during your discussion with your parents.

Euphemisms can work to your advantage here too. When trying to open a conversation about estate planning with your parents or other relatives, you may find it useful to avoid calling it a meeting about "making wills" and instead refer to it as a meeting about "planning for the future." That has a much more positive connotation. Try to keep the feeling of the meeting upbeat instead of gloomy by focusing on the positive outcomes you and your family will

achieve, such as peace of mind and a better understanding of what is important to each other.

Some of the openers you might use include:

- "Mom and Dad, I'd like to sit down with you sometime soon and find out whether you've taken legal steps to look after each other in the future."

- "I'd really like to know what your wishes are if you get sick. Let's talk about what you need to put into place to make sure things are done the way you want."

Be clear with your parents about the advantages they can expect from talking about estate planning and incapacity planning. Explain why you believe this is important for them. More than anything else, your parents must understand that even though you are the one initiating the planning or the family meeting, or both, the advantages of planning go to them, not to you.

Feel free to share the parts of this book with them that you feel will inform and motivate them.

## 2. Be Prepared for a Reaction

To bring up any obviously negative topic successfully, you need to put yourself in the shoes of the other person. Try putting yourself in the place of your parent and think about what it would be like to be told that you have become so frail or incompetent that you cannot look after yourself any longer. Nobody would welcome hearing that. It can be extremely upsetting and frightening for the person being given this news, and most people will put up quite a bit of resistance to the idea.

As adults, we cherish our freedom to live where we like, drive our cars when we feel like it, eat the food we like, and generally spend our time doing the things that we think are important or enjoyable. Many seniors perceive having someone else in charge of their affairs as giving up some or all of their independence and dignity.

You should be prepared to deal with emotional upset that might include fear, anger, sadness, denial, resentment, anxiety, or suspicion. If you expect these reactions, and do not let them derail you, you may be more prepared to stay calm and show compassion for the other person's situation. If this should happen, allow the upset person to have his or her say and try to determine what his or her real fears are. No matter what, stay calm. Reassure your parent that nobody is trying to take anything away from him or her, and that you are only bringing it up because you want to help.

The other reaction you might anticipate is that of your siblings or other family members who might be close with your parents. Not everyone is going to agree with what you want for your parents, so you might as well get used to that idea immediately. You cannot please everyone, and as has been mentioned many times in this book, the subject matter you are working with is delicate enough to ensure that you will hardly please anyone.

Many families find it hard to agree on what is best for a parent who needs help. Even when the solution is agreed upon, there is often dissent about how best to implement it. Do not fight with your siblings to the point that your parents become used as weapons in the battle. Keep your goal in mind. Your goal does not include upsetting your parents because the children are fighting.

If you and your family members are simply not going to see eye-to-eye, get a mediator involved. There are mediators who specialize in elder issues, but if one is not available in your area, find someone with experience with family issues. Remember that if you leave the suggestion of a mediator too late and your siblings are already furious with you, you might have lost your opportunity. Try to introduce the idea of a mediator before things get out of hand.

## 3. What Not to Say

While this book is about what to say, you might also think about what not to say. It is frustratingly easy to make mistakes with touchy subjects and doing so can sometimes send a small struggle spiraling into a huge dispute. You do have to be careful and think through what you will say and how you will say it before approaching your parents. The idea is to minimize upset.

Here are some things that you should *not* do when trying to motivate your parents or other family members into doing their estate planning. Many of them are simply common sense, but use this list to prepare yourself for your conversation:

- Do not be judgmental. For example, it is not a good idea to say that the fact that they have not done any planning shows that they are lazy, selfish, or negligent. Do not tell your parents that they are bad people or lousy parents for not taking care of their planning. Do not attempt to shame or embarrass them into action. Doing this is counterproductive and will only make people defensive, angry, or annoyed with you. Nobody is going to feel like cooperating with you if you are aggressive in this way, so it will not help you achieve your goal of encouraging your parents to do their planning. Try to put yourself in their position by understanding their worries and limitations.

- Do not frighten your parents by saying things like, "You could die tomorrow." This often has the effect of paralyzing a person into inaction, which is the opposite of what you intend. It may also upset or depress them.

- Do not threaten your parents. Do not threaten to cut them out of your life or to keep their grandchildren away from them if they refuse to get on with their planning. Those kinds of ultimatums are emotional blackmail. Also do not threaten them that if they do not take action, you will take matters out of their hands and force a solution on them. This will only make them angry and cause them to distrust you. After that they will likely keep their matters even more private from you.

- Do not make it about you. It is your parents' planning. While it is fair to make a general statement that estate planning is a gift to the loved ones left behind, including you, it is not fair to demand that they do this for you. Instead, encourage them to see the advantages for themselves, their business, or farm (if they own one), and the family as a whole.

- Do not give false or misleading information in an attempt to scare or trick your parents into action. There is an abundance of false material out there, such as myths about how the government will automatically take a person's estate if he or she does not have a will. However, your parents will eventually learn the truth when they consult a lawyer and they will not trust you after they realize that you have misled them.

- Do not be impatient. Let your parents take the time they need to mull over

matters, consider options, ask questions, or read about certain subjects. Estate planning involves important decisions that should not be rushed. You may have to have several conversations with them before matters are settled. As long as they are actually working on it, let them move at their own pace.

## 4. Create a Safe Environment

A safe environment is one in which everyone feels comfortable talking about a subject because they know that nobody is going to attack or belittle them. If people are not going to express their real feelings or worries, or are going to withhold information, then the conversation is really not worth having.

Do your best to make sure that your parents are confident that they will not be bullied, ridiculed, pressured, or ignored during the discussion. Family dynamics unfortunately often result in one person's opinions being trampled by others, or arguments erupting. Even if nobody is being treated this way by the others, the person may fear that he or she will be treated this way and refuse to participate.

Whenever you are talking about subjects that are difficult to begin with, you may have to go the extra mile to make sure that everyone is going to listen to each other respectfully and that nobody is afraid to participate. If it is your parent who is volatile, as opposed to you being volatile, it is a good idea to raise this point up front and state that everyone is expected to stay calm and hear each other out.

Before starting a conversation or meeting, turn off your cell phone, BlackBerry, iPhone, or iPod, and ask your parents to do the same. Ask them for their full attention for a few minutes while you have this conversation. It is a lot easier for your parents to agree to have a meeting and to give you their full attention if the conversation or meeting is being held at a time when they are not expected to be at work, eating a meal, or asleep.

A big part of the comfort level for your parents in a conversation like this will come from you being respectful of your parents' wishes and concerns. Understand that plenty of parents resist this kind of conversation because they fear they will be pressured or ignored by their children. They can be afraid that if they agree to talk about their future ability to live alone, for example, they might suddenly find themselves dropped off at the door of a long-term care facility.

It is important for you to reassure your parents that the purpose of the conversation is to find out what they need so that other people (including yourself) are not imposing unwanted help on them. The purpose is for you to listen. The intent is not to interfere with their independence, but to find out what help or support they really want or need from you and other family members.

## 5. The More You Talk, the Easier It Gets

We have already mentioned that many people are uncomfortable talking about planning for someone they love's or their own death or incapacity. Sometimes people simply cannot get through planning meetings without tears because the topics are upsetting. When you bring up estate planning with your parents, anticipate that they may have this reaction. Stay calm and professional, and be as reassuring as you can.

It may be a good idea to bring up the topic more than once, on separate days. The first time, bring it up just long enough for your parents to agree in principle to talk about

planning. At the same time, agree on when you will get together again to talk about it. For example, you might bring up the topic and then say something like, "Why don't we get together Saturday afternoon at three o'clock to talk about it?" In this way, you have broken the ice on the topic but you are not forcing anyone to sit down and deal with it right away, when they may be unprepared to make important decisions.

When you then come back on the Saturday afternoon (or whatever date you have arranged), you will find it easier to talk about the topic because it has already been mentioned once. People will have had a chance to prepare themselves mentally, think about their issues, write a list of questions, or do some research. After the first mention, the topic becomes a little less intimidating. Each subsequent mention of estate and incapacity planning will be easier than the last.

## 6. Agree to Try Things

Imagine how helpless and distressed your parents might feel if you demand that they leave their home for good, move into an unfamiliar facility that they did not even get to choose, or accept a stranger into their home as a caregiver. You would not like it if it were you, so there is no reason to expect that anyone else would. It is no surprise that aging parents resist these major life changes over which they have no control.

The changes might not seem so frightening or overwhelming if your parent has your promise that if he or she tries an arrangement for a few weeks, you will agree to review and reassess the arrangement at that time. It is essential that your parent knows you are listening to his or her concerns and that if the arrangement is one in which the parent is mistreated, neglected, or simply cannot tolerate for any reason, you are there to help and protect the parent by finding a better arrangement.

Sometimes the situation you have arranged for your parent is not at all ideal, but it is the best option open to you and your parent. Options can be limited by finances, by geography, or by a dozen other factors. If your arrangement is less than ideal, agree to review it in a few weeks if your parent will agree to give it an honest try for now. That is the best that either of you can do at present. You have to trust each other to stick to your word about this arrangement.

Keep the lines of communication open during the trial period. Arrange a time and a means of communication and stick to it. For example, will you phone every evening? Will you drop by twice a week? Both of you should be clear about how and when you will discuss things. As a word of caution, make sure your parent knows that if he or she is frightened or mistreated, he or she does not have to wait until the prearranged time to contact you. Also make sure that the review you promised does actually take place.

## 7. How to Bring up Incapacity

Talking to your parent about his or her diminishing capacity is going to take tact and patience. Do not be abrupt when telling your parent that you think he or she is beginning to lose mental capacity. None of us likes to be told what to do, and nobody likes personal criticism, particularly if it is said in a cruel, demanding, or belittling way. Deliver the message in a way that shows that you care about your parent and are concerned about his or her well-being.

For example, if you believe that it is no longer a good idea for your parent to be driving a car because of impaired memory, confusion, slowed reflexes, or other problems related to cognition, do not say:

- "You almost drove over a kid on a bike! You're a menace! Your driving days are over, starting right now. I'm taking your keys away."

By speaking this way, you have accused your parent of doing something wrong and you have bullied him or her as well. None of this is going to make your parent feel like cooperating with you. In fact, many people will become stubborn when spoken to this way and will dig in their heels on an issue rather than listen to your point of view. Instead of using abusive, accusatory language, try something like the following two statements:

- "I've noticed lately that driving isn't as easy for you as it used to be. I'm worried about your safety. Let's talk about it."

- "I have some information about a service that specializes in transporting seniors to appointments and shopping. Would you like to see it and talk about whether you'd enjoy having the service drive you?"

The approach is the same when addressing the idea that a parent can no longer live alone due to memory problems or confusion. Do not say:

- "You forgot to pay the phone bill again, didn't you? What's wrong with you? Maybe it's time you moved to a long-term care facility."

When phrased like that, moving to a long-term care facility sounds more like punishment than a solution to a problem. Again, the tone is accusing and rough. Rather than put your parent on the defensive, try saying the following:

- "I know you're forgetting things lately. I'm worried about you living on your own. Let's sit down with a cup of tea and talk about whether we should make some changes."

This kind of phrasing sounds like you are there to help, not accuse. You seem cooperative rather than bullying. You are leaving some or all of the decision-making authority with your parent. Your motivation sounds like concern, not a need to punish the person for bad behavior.

# What to Say or Do to Get Your Parents Motivated and Moving

Often children who want their parents to do some planning are willing to talk to their parents about it. They have informed themselves as to the pros and cons of estate planning and are convinced that it is important for their parents. However, they do not bring it up because they do not know how to do so in a way that will motivate the parents into taking action. They are not going to waste time talking to deaf ears.

How do they get their parents to realize that estate planning is not just for other people but is important for them too? How do they convince their parents that it is something they should do and can do?

In this chapter, we will look at some specific ideas on what you can say to open up conversations with your family members. We will look

at a number of common situations — such as funerals, or a friend moving in with his or her adult children — that are natural springboards to the discussion you need to have. We will also look at other ideas for triggering that discussion, such as hearing about celebrity estates. There are things going on around you and your parents right now that you can draw on for motivation.

There are some specific wordings given in this chapter, which you may be able to adapt to your situation. Not all ideas fit all families, but no doubt you will find at least two or three ideas here that you can use immediately.

## 1. Celebrity Estates

Whenever a famous or important person dies, the media report in minute detail about the deceased person, the estate itself, and the re-action of family and friends. If there is any kind of dispute going on with the estate, that too will be revealed and analyzed. From time to time, the media bring readers and viewers a story about an estate that has ended up in court and we watch as the messy tale unfolds.

The same kinds of disputes happen to those of us who are not famous or rich. While our lives may not be recorded on camera for the world to see as theirs are, the same issues arise. Children are sometimes not treated equally and the one who is left out wants to know why. One person is given something that another person thought he or she should get instead. There is suspicion that the deceased person was influenced by someone. The will is unclear about who gets what, or there is no will at all. The person who died had a blended family of children and stepchildren and nobody is sure who is supposed to be included. There is less money in the estate than expected and the family wants to know where it went.

All of these things can and do happen to or-dinary people as well as to celebrities. Anyone's estate can end up being just as big a mess for the loved ones left behind. Though our stories are not always splashed across the media for all to see, the issues are the same and the im-pact on the family members is just as painful. Therefore we can look at these celebrity estates as a way of beginning a conversation about some of the nasty things that can happen when people fail to plan for their eventual deaths.

The stories in the media can be used to your advantage as a means to encourage your parents or other relatives to get on with their estate planning, as they illustrate what can happen. If your parent has not already seen or heard the latest news or gossip about a fa-mous person's disastrous estate, tell him or her about it. Then use it as a springboard into a

conversation about how this estate is an ex-ample of what can happen if people do not take the time to plan ahead properly.

You can use phrases such as the following:

- "I want to make sure nothing terrible like that happens in our family."

- "We can protect our family from having to go through something like that."

- "I know you don't want any of us to go through that."

Sometimes the immediacy of seeing a celeb-rity's bereaved or bewildered family member's face right in your own living room on your tele-vision screen can bring the issues to the fore-front. We watch because the face on the screen is familiar, and the issue then becomes familiar as well. It is hard to ignore the fact that some-one made a huge mistake such as not making a will, when it is repeatedly flashed in front of us in full color every night on the news. Use the popularity of celebrities to your advantage when you are trying to motivate someone who simply does not seem to want to get started.

Sometimes an estate is in the news simply because the will does something that seems unusual to the general public. For example, most of us have heard news stories about wills that left millions of dollars to the family pet or bypassed the children in favor of a charity. Cases like this generate a lot of publicity and there is always a lot of talk in particular about why the deceased person made the choice that he or she did.

People wonder about the dynamics be-tween the deceased person and the spouse or children who were left with nothing. There is always speculation especially when the person bypassed immediate family members or other logical recipients of the money. This gets people thinking about what they would have done in that person's place, which is exactly what you want your parents to think about.

This can be a very good jumping-off point for talking about why it is necessary for wills to be properly done. The logical opening sentence is that the unusual gift (such as that made to a charity rather than children) could not and would not have happened if the person had not made a will. This will also easily lead into a discussion of how important it is that families understand what is happening in a will so that nobody is tempted to contest it.

You could start a conversation with the following:

- "If he hadn't had a good will, that money would have gone to his ex-wife (or other individual, depending on the circumstances), which isn't what he wanted. Everyone should have a strong will like that."

- "Nobody knows why she did that, but she had her reasons and it's her money so it should go where she wants it to go."

- "You mentioned that you are hoping to leave some money to your favorite charity when you pass away. Have you had that put into a will yet?"

Many wills are contested on the basis that the person making the will and giving his or her money to an animal shelter or church or charity must be mentally incapacitated. The argument of those contesting the will rests on the idea that giving the money to the family pet (instead of to them) is so crazy that nobody in their right mind would do it. On the face of it, that might seem like a pretty good case to contest the will.

However, if the will is properly made up by a wills lawyer, he or she will make sure there is evidence in the file as to why the decision was made and that the person making the will was of sound mind at the time. For example, the lawyer, who is trained to test each person making a will for capacity, will put a note in the file saying how and when he or she tested the individual and why he or she believes the person to be capable of making a will. Sometimes letters are also requested from doctors to back up the lawyer's assessment that the person in question was perfectly in possession of all faculties.

Making a will is the only way to make sure that an unusual wish can be directed to take place. If your parent has ever expressed a wish to make provision for the family pets, to give to a charity, or to do anything other than leave everything to the children, you may be able to use a famous estate example to draw attention to the importance of your parent making a will.

## 2. Messy Estate of Someone You Know

For those who do not feel that the lives of the rich and famous bear any resemblance to those of ordinary people such as themselves, it might be more effective to find an example of "what not to do" by looking at other family members, neighbors, and friends. Unfortunately, many estates do end up being contested due to poor will planning, mistakes, or simply unclear instructions so examples are everywhere. Everyone can recount at least the basics of a family or neighborhood story about an estate gone completely wrong.

Similar to looking at celebrity estates, it is possible to make something positive out of other people's unfortunate errors when we use them as reminders to take care of our own families. You might, for example, have a relative or friend who everyone thought was well off but left no money behind, and his widow lost the house to creditors. You might know someone whose children contested the will and changed what the person had originally intended to do with his or her estate. Perhaps you have heard stories about children left without guardians, businesses failing for lack of cash, or houses taken for tax debts.

People's lives are complicated and so are their estates after they pass away. You might be able to use these situations to try to motivate your parents to do a better job than the unfortunate friend or neighbor who did not plan properly and left his or her family in the lurch.

You might want to try the following statements when talking to your parents:

- "Mr. Smith is really having a tough time now that his wife has passed away. Too bad she didn't leave a will. I hope you have made a will yourself so that this doesn't happen in our family."

- "The McIsaac kids are fighting over who gets their mother's estate and some of them are saying they'll never speak to their siblings again. I hope you'll leave a will so we'll know what you want us to do."

- "It looks like Janet is going to lose the house because her husband never did change that life insurance policy to name her. I hope you and Dad have taken care of all of that."

# 3. Life Event Triggers

Sometimes events occur in your life or your parents' lives that are good stepping-stones into discussions about planning. The following are a few examples of events that often trigger this conversation, though there could also be many more.

These triggers are effective and powerful because they are common events that could happen to you or to your parents at any time, and they have an immediacy that hits home. Each one of these triggers could start a conversation about "What if this happened to you?" because your parents see it happening around them.

## 3.1 Sudden illness

If an uncle has a heart attack and is in the hospital, it might be a good time to open a conversation about who is directing his health care while he is sick. You might then say to your parents something like the following:

- "If this happened to you, what would we do?"

- "Do you have a health-care directive so that someone could speak for you in an emergency?"

- "Who have you named as your health-care decision maker?"

If the reply is that no health-care directive exists, you might follow up by saying something like the following:

- "I believe that we would all have more peace of mind if we were sure we knew what your actual wishes are. Would you do that for us?"

- "Wouldn't you like to know that we are ready to help you out in an emergency and that the papers are in place for that?"

## 3.2 Going into long-term care

As your parents age, they will no doubt think about the idea that one or both of them might one day live in a long-term care facility. For most, that is a pretty frightening concept. They are worried about loneliness, living conditions, mistreatment, finances, and many other things.

If someone you know, or your parent knows, should go to live in a long-term care facility, you might mention it to your parent to gauge his or her reaction. If your parent responds with a statement that reveals his or her wishes, which could be anything from, "I don't ever want to live in an institution," to "It's a good idea for me to live there because I don't want to be a burden to my children," this would be a perfect opportunity to talk about planning for his or her future.

You could answer with something similar to the following statements:

- "You should make sure that your wishes are written down properly so that everyone will know what you want."

- "Among your children, we have very different ideas about whether you should live in long-term care. It would be a good idea for you to get your instructions put into a legal document so that we don't fight about it."

For almost everyone, a discussion of long-term care facilities and alternative living arrangements is closely tied to a discussion about finances, since the cost of care is an enormous factor. As the population ages, demand for good long-term care facilities will increase, likely driving prices even higher. On the topic of paying for care, you might start a conversation with the following:

- "Have you ever wondered if you'd be able to afford to pay for long-term care if you ever need it? Maybe you and I should look into it so that we know what it costs?"

- "I've heard of this type of insurance that pays if you go to live in long-term care. We should compare the price of it to the cost of long-term care to see if it's a good idea."

## 3.3  Funeral of a family member or friend

All of our lives go through stages where groups of our contemporaries are getting married or having children or grandchildren. Unfortunately, there also comes a stage of life in which many of our peers are passing away. You will find that as you get older, you attend more funerals of family and friends. Your parents might be at that stage. You will often hear seniors mentioning how many people they knew who have recently passed away.

Though this is obviously not a happy occasion, the fact that your parent might be quite aware of his or her own mortality is very useful in motivating him or her to take action on his or her own estate planning. Some openers that you can use to get your parent talking about wills and will planning include:

- "I heard that this funeral was carried out exactly as Aunt Marie wanted. Have you put anything in writing about what you want when your time comes?"

- "Going to this funeral makes me realize that one day it will be my turn so I am going to look at my will to see if it is up to date. Why don't you do that too?"

## 3.4  Getting married (again) later in life

When someone you know marries for the second (or third or more) time, the issues surrounding blended families crop up. The marriage that triggers an estate-planning conversation does not have to be someone in your immediate family. It could be a neighbor or extended family member or a close friend.

The issues surrounding blended families tend to involve figuring out how to look after so many people with competing interests. For example, how to make sure that the children from the first marriage and those from the second marriage are all looked after financially.

If you see someone marry for the second time trying to blend everyone into a workable group, you wonder how he or she is juggling so many legal rights.

Another issue is whether stepchildren are to be included in any inheritance under a will. This is something that many people overlook, simply by using the word "children" in a will, or worse, not making a will at all.

A concern voiced by many individuals is that a spouse will make a will leaving everything to a second spouse and nothing to the children; the person dies leaving all to the new spouse who then remarries, and the children never do get anything financially under the parent's will.

When someone you know or your parents know gets married for the second time, you can use this as a springboard to a conversation about the importance of wills. You could say something like the following:

- "Susan had that house before she married Jim. She told me she wants her kids to own it one day. I hope she makes a will to make sure that happens."

- "Cathy doesn't get along with Fred's children from his first marriage. I hope Fred is taking care of his will so that Cathy never gets caught in the middle of a fight."

- "Do you have a will in place so we know what you want to have happen?"

## 3.5 Losing mental faculties

There may be a friend or relative in your life or your parent's life who is beginning to lose mental capacity, or who is already fully in the grips of memory loss and confusion. It becomes obvious very quickly that a person in that situation needs a lot of support and assistance.

If you see, for example, your Uncle Zeno struggling with Alzheimer's disease, you might also notice his daughter, your cousin Maggie, helping out. The help might be moving Uncle Zeno to a new residence, arranging for meals to be brought to him, taking him to medical appointments, or taking over his banking. You can use this situation to illustrate your parent's future needs by saying something like the following:

- "It's a good thing Maggie knows what her father wants. Do you have any documents saying what you'd want in that situation?"

- "Who would you want to look after you in this situation? Do you have a health-care document with your wishes written down?"

- "Uncle Zeno doesn't have a will and it's too late for him to make one now. It looks like there might be a fight shaping up between Maggie and her brother. Please make sure you have documents in place to prevent that happening to us."

## 3.6 Friend moves in with his or her adult children

Occasionally your parent will have a friend or relative about the same age who sells the family home and moves in with one of his or her children. This may be an arrangement made instead of moving into long-term care, or it might be done for purely economic reasons.

If your parent mentions that a friend has done this or is in the process of doing this, you might ask:

- "Would you want to live with one of us? If so, which one?"

- "If you had to move, would you rather live with one of us kids or in a long-term care facility?"

- "Have you ever written down your wishes in a legal document so that everyone knows how you feel about this?"

# 4. Do Your Own Planning

One of the gentlest, but also most effective, ways to motivate your parents or other family members to take care of their estate planning is to do your own planning and then share your experiences with them. Once you are in the process of your own planning, mention it to your parents in a casual way. You might mention, for example, that you have an appointment coming up with a lawyer, or that you will be seeing your investment advisor to get updated information for the planning session.

Explain what you expect to gain from the process, such as peace of mind that your family will be looked after. Tell your parents the reasons you had for getting your planning done and out of the way.

Once you have completed the process and your documents are finished, you could invite your parents to go through the process as well. Let them know that it was not as intimidating or difficult as you had expected, or that it took less time than you had anticipated.

You might say something like the following:

- "I'm really glad that is done. I have a lot more peace of mind. You should do the same yourselves."

- "That really was a great process and much easier than I thought it would be. You really should do it yourselves. Do you want my lawyer's number?"

- "The lawyer had some fantastic ideas for my will that I hadn't even thought of. I'm so happy with the result. It was a really worthwhile experience. You should make an appointment for yourself."

## 4.1 Blame it on your lawyer

If you simply have not been able to bring up the subject of estate planning at all because you do not want to be the author of the idea, try putting the onus on the professionals looking after your own estate planning. For example, you might say that you are beginning your own estate planning and because of that, your lawyer or accountant wants to know what is in place for the previous generation.

This will no doubt give rise to several questions by your parents, but you should be able to explain to them how the financial issues and legal issues of one family member can impact on another.

If you choose to go this route, you will be able to deflect any blame or criticism from your parents or other family members about being greedy, cold, or controlling.

# 5. Travel

Making new wills before traveling has become very popular. After the events of September 11, 2001, there was a steep spike in the number of people who wanted to make wills before traveling by air, and it has not slowed down. Though most people do not dwell on what could happen to them, there is a general awareness and acceptance these days that we should be prepared for the unexpected. Part of that is an awareness that we need to prepare wills before traveling.

The willingness to make wills before traveling seems just as prevalent among people who are traveling by train, car, or boat as it is among those traveling by air. These days making wills is as much a part of preparing for vacation as getting a passport, hiring a pet sitter, and locking the doors.

Most people who have been aware of the need to do estate planning but who have been putting it off can see the logic in making documents at that point in time. This is particularly true if they are traveling outside of their own country. They like the idea that if they do not make it back home, everything is nicely in order. Many comment that it will be hard enough on the children to get the news of their demise without the children also having to hear that there is a legal mess for them to clear up as well.

You can use this situation to motivate your parents if they are planning any travel in the near future or if they like to spend the winter in a warmer climate. Let them know that it makes sense to put all of their affairs in order before leaving on that cruise or getaway so that they can relax and enjoy the trip. The best thing about using this particular motivator is that it has nothing to do with your parents' ages or finances or possible frailties. The urgency is not really about them; most adults on the airplane probably have a will, whether or not they are seniors.

Ideally, you should urge your parents to contact an estate-planning lawyer about three weeks or a month before they plan to travel, to make sure that the documents can be prepared, reviewed, fine-tuned, and signed before it is time to leave for vacation. Many people leave this too late and only call the lawyer a day or two before leaving, ensuring that either they do not get a will at all, or they get one that is hastily thrown together.

## 6. Help with Research

If your parents or family members have agreed that they do need to do some planning but simply do not know where to start, help them find the information or help they need.

This is not as simple as taking them to your own lawyer, sitting in on the meeting to tell the lawyer what they want, and then leaving. In fact, this might not be a good idea at all. This scenario can cause a lot of problems if it appears that you are influencing your parents to put in their wills what you want them to put in, or that you are having them change their documents to your advantage.

The following are some ideas for gathering reliable information about estate planning, both in general and to address specific topics.

Look around for seminars that your parents can attend, either with you or on their own. Helping them make important decisions about their estates is probably worth paying for a seminar, but it is not impossible to find free ones. To find seminars, check out some of the following ideas:

- Look at the websites or brochures put out by your local library, as seminars offered through libraries are often free of charge. These seminars are usually held in the evenings or on weekends so that people with daytime jobs are able to attend them.

- Check into organizations that deal with seniors' issues to see whether they offer any seminars. The organizations you might check with include nonprofit groups and associations that deal with retirement, semiretirement, seniors' housing, seniors' advocacy, Alzheimer's disease, and aging gracefully.

- Check continuing education classes offered by colleges or high schools. Look for one-day or one-evening sessions that deal specifically with estate planning, preferably for seniors. The sessions might be called estate planning, will planning, or even retirement planning.

- If there is a law school nearby, check whether it has a student law clinic, as often the clinical programs will offer free or low-cost public sessions. Keep in mind that if you use this option, the person advising you will be a student who has the academic background to help you but does not have any experience in a real-life setting as of yet.

- If your parents are business owners, check out business organizations that are intended to educate and assist their members. These are usually nonprofit organizations, though there are paid membership organizations as well. They are not marketing sites, but advertise themselves as a source of information, education, or other resources. Frequently these organizations publish excellent articles on their websites in addition to offering seminars that you can either attend in person or attend by way of podcast.

- Look at the websites for local trust companies and larger banks to see whether they offer any sessions. Make sure you ask whether you have to already be a customer to attend. These are unlikely to be free of charge, but they will be very focused on estate-planning steps that you need to take.

To find materials other than seminars, try these ideas:

- Read library books on elder law, elder issues, legal aspects of aging, retirement planning, or estate planning.

- Check out literature that is sent around by large charities such as community foundations, seniors' advocacy groups, or retirement-planning groups.

- Look at the websites for local governments as often they have quite a bit of free information posted for download, or will provide you with brochures at no cost.

- Look at the websites for law firms in your local area to see whether they offer articles or podcasts. If you are using a search engine to find law firms, try searching "estate planning for seniors" together with the name of your city or town.

- Check out free literature offered by local probate courts. This type of information tends to be very practical and useful, as long as you know which specific task you want to do (e.g., prepare a will, probate a will).

- Browse through the self-help, how-to, legal, and family sections of your local bookstore. Choose books that are easy for nonlawyers to read and understand; otherwise, nobody will actually use the information in the book. You should read the book yourself before giving it to your parents to read.

- If you note a speaker or lecturer on estate planning has put on a talk that you did not attend but would have found useful, search the Internet for more information about the speaker. You might just discover that the speaker has a blog or book with more information.

- Read magazines that are designed for people aged 50 or older. As the population ages, there is a virtual explosion of these magazines that deal with all aspects of life for seniors. Most contain up-to-date information about estate planning and other legal topics of interest to people in that age bracket. If you read a magazine article that you particularly enjoy, look at the author information to see whether it is someone local that you could contact on behalf of your parents.

In addition to doing the kinds of research described above, there are other information-gathering steps you can take. For example, if your parent is considering selling his or her home and moving into a long-term care facility, go and see some of the facilities. Make appointments if possible, and take your parent around to see the facilities, the grounds and amenities, the staff, the location, and the accessibility. Also find out the cost.

## 7. Reassurance

Whichever specific method you use to bring up a topic, make sure you communicate to your parents how the proposed arrangement is in their best interests. A little bit of reassurance goes a long way toward establishing and maintaining trust between you and your parents. Use specific examples of incidents or situations in their lives that could have been avoided had the new arrangement been in place.

For example, you might have concluded that your parent should move to a long-term care facility and you are wondering how to talk to him or her about that. Most individuals who place an elderly parent in a long-term care facility do so with an almost overwhelming sense of guilt. They feel as if they should look after their parents themselves but resort to long-term care facilities when it becomes clear that they cannot provide the care, attention, and supervision needed.

Once you begin your conversation, share these reasons with your parents. For example, help them understand that moving in with you would not be a viable option because if you are at work all day, there is nobody at home to help with meals, toileting, and medication. Reassure your parents that you will still be involved in their life.

The purpose in sharing your reasons with your parent is not to reduce your guilt, but to reassure your parent that all reasonable options were explored and that this proposed arrangement is the best suited to your parent's needs.

# Acting without a Parent's Agreement

We have spent a great deal of time in this book talking about motivating your parents to take care of their own planning. However, sometimes it is simply too late for them to do their own planning and you may not be able to prevent that. You should realize that there might be a time when you must act on behalf of your parent, whether he or she invites that or not. This refers to a time when your parent is suffering from memory loss or dementia, which makes it impossible for him or her to continue to make reasonable decisions.

The condition of not being able to make reasonable decisions for yourself is called *incapacity*. Once your parents no longer have capacity, they cannot sign legal documents giving anyone authority over their assets. If they have not signed documents, you are likely to be acting without their agreement simply because

they no longer have the mental capacity required by law for them to give consent.

Should this set of circumstances exist in your family, you will find that it is a major turning point. Once deterioration of mental faculties begins, it tends to worsen over time, and eventually your parent could reach the point where he or she is no longer able to do any planning for himself or herself. Once your parent is incapacitated, he or she is vulnerable in many ways, both financially and physically. You or another family member will likely have to take legal steps to protect your parent, whether or not your parent wants you to.

As a word of caution, do not assume that capacity has been lost without confirmation from a doctor. There could be other explanations for the symptoms shown by your parent, so make sure you do not jump the gun in concluding that your parent has lost his or her capacity. It can only be fair to your parent to be sure of this diagnosis before you begin legal steps based on it. If your parent has a family doctor that knows him or her well, that is a good place to start. If you need to see a specialist in geriatrics, or another specialist of some kind, your family doctor can set you on the right track.

If possible, try to get the doctor's diagnosis of incapacity in writing. This is because you might find that when you bring up the subject of a parent's mental incapacity, each and every family member will have a slightly (or possibly widely) different perspective on it. Even if family members agree that there has been some deterioration, they are not likely to agree on how far it has progressed or how severe it is. Having a doctor do a written assessment that everyone can read helps to keep everyone's understanding and expectations of the situation in line. It also takes the heat off you, or any other family member who is promoting the idea that your parent is beginning to experience deterioration.

Also understand that a parent may make decisions that you personally do not like or agree with, but this does not mean that he or she is incapacitated. It just means that you have different views on a subject. The idea of acting on behalf of a parent, with or without that parent's agreement, is to help the person and to act on his or her behalf (Chapter 1 addresses this in more detail). It is not intended as a way for you to prevent your parents from taking steps that you do not like. Incapacity documents should only be used to assist and never to control.

As mentioned earlier, capacity tends to diminish over time. It is rarely the case that a person loses all of his or her capacity instantly, unless there is a major injury or trauma of some sort. In the early stages of memory loss, it may still be possible for your parent to do his or her planning, though at that point there is some urgency. If at all possible, you should make sure that your parent has the opportunity to do his or her own estate planning and not take that right and opportunity away from him or her.

## 1. In the Parent's Best Interest

If you are in a situation where your parent cannot make decisions for himself or herself and you step in to handle legal and financial matters, you will likely be required to go through the courts to ask for the legal authority you need. You may be appointed as a *trustee* for financial matters or a *guardian* for personal and health matters, or you might be appointed to both of those jobs.

In this situation, you are required to act in the best interests of your parent, even if doing so goes against your own best interests. This is the cornerstone of your legal authority and it must be the basis of every decision you make as a guardian and/or trustee. It is a hard standard for most people to meet and you should consider whether it is realistic for you to take on a role that requires that kind of selflessness from you.

Once you begin acting on behalf of your parent, you may be faced with the difference between what your parent wants and what is best for him or her in any given situation. You will have to figure out what to do, and that is not easy when your parent is not cooperating.

The most common example of this dilemma is the one in which a parent is adamant that he or she is going to continue to live in his or her house and not move to a long-term care facility. People insist on staying in their homes and refuse to understand that because they are widowed and living alone, and because their health is declining (e.g., eyesight, hearing, mobility), they are vulnerable. If they should fall, there is nobody there to help them up or call an ambulance. If there is a fire, they might not be able to get out of the house quickly. They may be losing the ability to shop for or prepare food, keep the house clean, or look after their own hygiene.

There frequently comes a time when a concerned child has to remove a parent from his or her home to a long-term care facility against the parent's wishes, simply because it just is not safe for the parent to live alone any longer. This is an incredibly difficult and upsetting decision for the child to make, particularly if the parent protests and resists. The child can be overwhelmed with feelings of guilt even while knowing it is the right thing to do for the parent. In this situation, the child has to do what is best for the parent, even though it is not what the parent wants him or her to do.

A similar problem can arise when you have to insist that your parent can no longer drive. Having the car keys taken away is a huge loss of independence for many seniors and many will, understandably, fight the loss of their own transportation very fiercely. Unfortunately it may be clear to everyone else on the road that your parent cannot drive any longer, while your parent may be oblivious to the problem. Again, the feelings of guilt can be overwhelming if you cause your parent such unhappiness when your goal is only to keep him or her safe.

If you are considering becoming a trustee for your parent's financial affairs, first ask yourself whether you have any business or financial dealings with your parent. If you do, can you carry out your duties as a trustee in the best interest of your parent and not in your own best interest?

For example, you might receive an occasional loan or financial handout from your parent in tough financial times. Perhaps your parent does not always insist that you pay it back because he or she is trying to help you out. Think about the position this puts you in if you are a trustee of your parent's finances. Giving yourself a loan or handout (which in most places is unlawful in any event) is in your own best interest, but not in the best interest of your parent. Would you be able to conduct yourself strictly on your parent's behalf even if it meant you had to forego financial help?

## 2. What to Do to Reduce Stress

If you are proceeding with legal documents or a court application designed to give you legal authority over your parent's personal or financial affairs (read section **3.** for clarification on legal authority), then you are already dealing with your parent's loss of capacity. That in itself is a stressful situation as you try to adjust to your parent's newly diminished set of skills. Seeing a loved one lose memories and motor functions can be devastating.

Individual steps or tasks within the overall task of looking after your parent are also very stressful, as they can be emotional and confusing. The following are some examples of stressful steps you might have to take:

- Taking your parent for a mental assessment that he or she does not want to have.

- Taking away credit cards.

- Hiring a caregiver, housekeeper, or nurse your parent does not like.

- Insisting that your parent stay overnight in the hospital for treatment or tests.

- Putting your parent on a budget.

- Selling your parent's home or cottage.

Your parent who is the subject of all of this activity is going to find the situation extremely stressful. This level of anxiety is not helpful to anyone and may impair your ability to communicate with your parent. In fact, it may even cause health problems for your parent. You should do all that you can to keep everyone calm and the lines of communication open.

The following are some ideas for trying to keep your parent's level of anxiety and disorientation at a minimum:

- Involve your parent in the decision-making process to the extent that he or she can handle. This level of involvement is different for everyone and you will have to assess the person's ability to function. While your parent might not be able to handle, for example, the documentation and financial transactions that are part of the sale of a home, he or she may still be perfectly capable of deciding which personal items in the home he or she wants to keep. If you exclude your parent from being involved in decisions that directly affect him or her, while he or she is capable of participating, you should expect that parent to be angry, resentful, or hurt just as any individual would be. This is not the way to get cooperation. Nor is it the way to deal respectfully with your parent.

- Keep your parent and your siblings informed as to steps that you have taken on your parent's behalf. Proactively giving out information is going to prevent you getting telephone calls and email messages constantly and having to repeat the same information to several people. For example, if you had agreed to see if the estate-planning lawyer would assist your parent, let everyone know that you have set up an appointment. Because your parent is the person who is the focus of the situation, you should keep him or her up-to-date personally if at all possible. If that is not possible, you should let him or her know by telephone. For other family members, consider options that will save you time and effort. For example, you could set up a distribution list on your email program that would include all family members with one click.

You could set up a private Facebook page or web page for your family so that everyone can be kept up to date by logging on to that page at their convenience.

If you do not wish to use the computer for your main means of communication, consider setting up a telephone-tree arrangement in which you ask each person you call to call two or three others and pass your message along. That will greatly reduce the number of calls you have to make. A telephone tree can be set up in advance so that everyone knows who they have to call if there is news to be distributed.

- While you are dealing with your parent, either privately or in the company of advisors and family members, be professional and calm. Give the appearance of being completely in control, even if you do not always feel that you are. If you are an emotional wreck, your distress will rub off on your parent. This will only make things worse, as your parent could be frightened about matters if you cry or break down every time estate planning is mentioned. He or she will wonder what terribly upsetting information you are hiding. If your parent is confused on any details, your distress will cause him or her to give the most negative interpretation possible to the issue.

- If you are acting on behalf of your parent on financial matters, make sure that anyone who becomes involved, such as appraisers, realtors, accountants, bankers, and lawyers know that they should contact you and not your parent. Give each person a photocopy of the document that gives you legal authority. Ensure that everyone knows that they must deal with you and not your parent.

  This is not intended to make you hide things from your parent; this arrangement is made so that your parent does not have strangers calling him or her to ask private financial information or to talk about unknown transactions. If your parent were capable of handling that situation, you would not be involved as his or her representative in the first place.

- If your parent asks you questions, answer them. Help your parent understand what you are doing and why you are doing it. When he or she wants to see documents, even if it is for the tenth time, show your parent the documents. Make sure bank statements, court documents, and letters from the lawyer are all kept in an orderly, acceptable place where they are safe and accessible and make it obvious that you have information at your fingertips that you can look up to answer your parent's questions. Write down information for him or her and display it in likely places, such as the front of the fridge where your parent can find it.

  Remember that aging parents are often experiencing memory loss and do not always realize they have asked the same question many times before. You can prevent this from becoming a stressful situation by simply being patient and answering it again.

- Listen to your parent if he or she wants to talk about his or her wishes. You may not always be able to carry out those wishes, for various reasons as discussed earlier in this chapter, but you should still know what your parent would like to have happen. The effect of having someone listen carefully to his or her plans and wishes and take the person seriously can have a very soothing effect. If you refuse to listen to your parent by saying something like, "Why should I listen? You're only going to forget what you said and tell me again tomorrow," you are only going to upset your parent and increase the stress level.

- Always be as gentle with your parents as you can. Remember that they are much more vulnerable now than they were when they were younger and rely on you much more than they used to. They are dependent on you and it is up to you to help them as humanely as possible.

Remember to work on your own stress level as well. People who provide care for their aging parents can do too much for their own health, particularly if they are also taking care of their children and/or a job at the same time. If you find that you are always exhausted, that you are catching numerous colds each year, or that you are depressed, it could be that you are overdoing it and need some relief.

Take breaks if you can. If there is nobody in your family who can help you with caring for your parents, you might look into hiring a caregiver for a certain portion of each day, or for a certain day a week. This will give you a chance to rest. You might also have to consider other living arrangements that have a greater level of support available.

# 3. Legal Authority

If you or another family member is going to begin looking after your aging parent, you are going to need legal authority to do so. Obviously you could move into your parent's home, or vice versa, without any legal permission from a third party to do so. You could help with meals, hygiene, housekeeping, and a dozen other matters without anyone else being involved.

However, once you want to deal with matters outside the home, or to have someone come in to help inside the home, you must have proper legal authority in place. Outside agencies such as banks, hospitals, and tax offices are not going to allow just anyone who comes in to deal with private or legal matters. You will need to prove that you have the right to do the transactions you are trying to do.

You will need legal authority for several reasons, including:

- Gaining access to private information about your parent's health records at the doctor's office, hospital, or clinic.

- Gaining access to private financial information at banks, insurance companies, investment houses, and the government's tax department.

- Signing documents on behalf of your parent at the bank or motor vehicle registry.

- Filing documents such as a tax return, house title transfer, or a contract for in-home care on behalf of your parent.

- Using your parent's money to pay his or her bills.

- Depositing checks to your parent's bank account.

- Investing or reinvesting your parent's money.

- Collecting money owed to your parent such as pensions, lawsuits, and inheritances.

- Selling items that your parent no longer wants, such as a vehicle, machinery, tools, or collections.

The steps to getting the proper legal authority in place include:

1. Find out if legal authority already exists. If so, no further steps are needed.

2. Find out whether your parent still has mental capacity to sign legal documents.

3. If legal documents can still be signed, get them signed.

4. If legal documents can no longer be signed due to loss of capacity, get court-ordered legal authority.

If you believe that your parent has lost capacity, and the doctor confirms this, your first step is to find out whether your parent has an enduring power of attorney already in place. If your parent already has that in place, the person named in the document will be able to step in and deal with matters on behalf of your parent. The enduring power of attorney document, together with a health-care directive, will give the person who is named the legal authority he or she needs. (To find out what other names an enduring power of attorney and health-care directive are called in different locations, see the Introduction.)

This chapter about acting without a parent's agreement has been based on the assumption that your parent has not put one of these documents in place and that there is nobody with legal authority to take care of matters for your parent. If you should discover that your parent has not put any documents of his or her own into place, you must next find out whether he or she can still do so. As mentioned earlier in this book, a person must have mental capacity to sign legal documents giving someone else control over his or her personal or financial affairs. If it is still possible for your parent to sign these documents, which allows him or her to make his or her own choices about who will be in charge and how things will be done, the documents should be done.

If you discover that your parent does not have mental capacity to sign important legal documents, you will likely have to approach the courts to become appointed as a legal guardian or trustee (the legal name for this role varies from place to place) for your parent.

For more information, see *Protect Your Elderly Parents: Become Your Parents' Guardian or Trustee,* another title published by Self-Counsel Press.

# Why Hold a
# Family Meeting?

If you are considering holding a family meeting, you may be wondering what you can hope to accomplish by doing so. What should you reasonably expect to result from holding a meeting? What will you, your parents, and your other family members really get out of it?

Obviously holding one meeting does not conclude everything. Your parents are not going to walk away from the meeting with an entire estate plan in place because they will still have to sign documents and meet with professionals after the meeting. That is assuming that everything could be resolved in one meeting, which is almost never the case. The following is what you can expect to accomplish at the first meeting:

- Bring interested family members together in a cooperative way.

- Make it clear that estate planning is important to the family as a group.

- Clarify your parent's wishes and goals.

- Help your parent understand that he or she is loved and protected.

- Let everyone have his or her say on issues that affect everyone.

- Find out who is willing to offer different kinds of help.

- Support each other in a crisis.

- Get agreement on steps to be taken.

- Become informed on issues such as a parent's failing health.

This chapter will give you some solid ideas about what kind of topics can and should be covered in a family meeting. Even if you may already be convinced that a family meeting is a good idea, you just might find out by reading this chapter that you can accomplish a lot more than you thought possible if your meeting is properly organized. This chapter will help you get the most out of a meeting.

## 1. Ensure That Your Parent's Wishes are Known, Understood, and Respected

A family meeting can be held to talk about anything that affects the whole family or a significant number of its members. We will concentrate on discussing family meetings that are held to talk about estate planning and related issues such as incapacity and finances.

The main reason for estate planning in general is to make a person's wishes known to his or her family members so that the person's wishes are carried out after his or her death. During a family meeting, those wishes can be expressed and documented. It is a chance for your parent to tell the family what he or she wants and to answer questions about plans to make sure that everyone understands the goals and the plans. He or she can get feedback if wanted, and can find out more information from children that might help finalize the wishes.

During a family meeting, there is an opportunity for plans that are only in the idea stage to be developed with the help of the family members. For example, a couple may have three grown children. The couple is trying to decide what they should do with their lake cottage, which during their lifetime is being used not only by them but by their children and grandchildren.

They are leaving their entire estate to their three children but are not sure whether they want to leave the title to the cottage in three names. They are worried about the children potentially arguing about who gets to use the cottage at any particular time, and maybe even about who should be paying for maintenance and repairs. They do not want to disappoint anyone who might be counting on continuing to use the cottage.

The couple raises the issue at a family meeting where all three children are attending. The couple asks their children what they want them to do with respect to the cottage. The oldest child says that she and her husband plan to buy their own cottage and do not need the parents' cottage. The middle child says that he is not particularly interested in spending time at the cottage. The younger child says that he and his wife would love to receive the cottage as part of his inheritance as his children are very interested in boating and swimming.

By asking for input from the family on this issue, the couple was able to finalize their plans for an important asset. You may be able to do the same with issues in your family.

## 2. Document the Wishes Properly and Legally

Once all of the plans have been decided and worked out in some detail, it is essential that they be properly documented. Otherwise it may be impossible for the plans to be carried out. The documents that everyone must have in place include an up-to-date will that appoints an executor and directs a distribution of assets after death. It is also absolutely essential to prepare documents that will support an individual who is still alive but who is suffering from physical deterioration or mental incapacity.

An enduring power of attorney (also called continuing power of attorney, durable power of attorney, or power of attorney for property, depending on where you live) will give a person the legal authority to deal with finances, property, taxes, assets, and debts on behalf of the aging parents. The person who will be put in charge is chosen by the parents and named in the document. This type of power of attorney is specially designed to be made ahead of time while a person is mentally healthy, and then brought into use at a later time when the person loses mental capacity.

To make decisions about health care, personal care, medical procedures, organ donation, and end-of-life issues, the aging person should have a health-care directive (also called advance directive, personal directive, power of attorney for health care, or health-care proxy). This document is not the same as a living will because it specifically names someone to be the decision maker and spokesperson for the aging person.

As with an enduring power of attorney, your parent will have the opportunity to pick someone he or she trusts as his or her representative. That person is named in the document and will be expected to step in and make decisions should your parent lose the ability to make personal and health decisions.

Whether or not your parent wants to use a lawyer to prepare documents will depend on a number of factors, including availability of lawyers and the cost. Some people can afford lawyers and have access to them but choose to take care of their own documents, as that is a personal choice. This is fine as long as your parent's affairs are as simple as he or she thinks they are.

There are some circumstances, which may not be considered simple, so your parents might want to think twice about preparing their own documents. They include:

- One or both of your parents is in a second or subsequent marriage, and there are children from the first marriage who are still minors.

- One of your parents is in a second marriage and the "first family" and "second family" do not always get along.

- Your parent owns a business or franchise.

- Your parent owns real estate in another country.

- Your parent owns a family farm.

- Your parents' financial affairs are complicated (e.g., joint-business ventures, holding companies, lease agreements).

## 3. Ease Anxieties

One of the main goals of estate planning is to provide peace of mind. This is obviously something to aim for with your parents. Your parents should be reassured that their children understand their wishes and are committed to carrying out those plans for them at the appropriate time. They should feel that they have reasonable, effective plans in place in the event that one of them loses capacity or passes away and that the family is prepared for those eventualities. There is a lot of comfort to be had just in knowing that everyone around them knows what to do in an emergency.

Your parents will also be relieved that with all the plans in place and all parties agreeing to them, there will not be fighting among the family members. The majority of people who state their goals for estate planning will say that more than anything, they want to prevent any quarrels among their children.

The rest of the family should find the process brings peace of mind as well. You should feel relief that your parents have turned their minds to preparing for eventualities. For example, you will know that in the event that one parent has a heart attack or stroke, plans are in place to keep things running. You will know that your parents' retirement funds are secure and are adequate to support them. From the family meeting you should gain enough information to feel that matters are under control and that there will not be financial or emotional struggles among family members.

## 4. Find Tax-Advantageous Solutions

While it is unlawful to evade paying taxes you legally owe, it is certainly legal to avoid paying more than you have to pay. Most people will agree that they would prefer to keep more of their estates in the pockets of their families and charities than they would in the coffers of the government. Deductions, tax shelters, and tax deferrals exist and are there for you to use, as long as you know about them and how to use them. Proper estate planning can make a difference of many thousands of dollars in taxes.

It is beyond the scope of this book to go into detail about how taxes can be minimized on estates. You should realize, however, that by talking things over with an estate-planning lawyer or an accountant, you are likely to hear about solutions that can be used to keep taxes to a minimum. You will also hear about ways to make sure that the estate has enough cash to pay the taxes that cannot be avoided. If you hold a family meeting, you might find it worthwhile to ask your lawyer or accountant to attend the meeting to talk about some of the tax-planning solutions.

The following are some of the ideas that can be explored with tax savings and tax payment:

- Trusts for title to property
- Trusts for spouses
- Family trusts
- Income-splitting trusts

- Trusts for shares of a business
- Assets put into joint names
- Life insurance policies to create cash flow
- Life insurance policies to insure debts or mortgages
- Designated beneficiaries on registered financial products

## 5. Preserve and Pass on Family Business or Farm

The majority of business owners are so busy working in their businesses and trying to grow and maintain them that they do not get around to making a business succession plan. This is not because they do not realize it needs to be done, but simply because they are busy with work, family, and other matters, and putting together a business succession plan can seem overwhelming.

It can be extremely difficult to pass on a business successfully, efficiently, and cost-effectively without any plans in place. Although many people assume that because their business is a family business it should be easier to pass the business on to the next generation, that is not necessarily the case.

If your parents own a business, some of the things that you and your family will talk about in your meeting will be general plans for the future of the business. For example, as a group you need to know who is going to be taking over the business in the future and in what role. If there is more than one person in the family who is interested in taking it over from your parents, you need to know what your parents want to do so that someone can make alternate plans.

You may find out that your parents want to distribute the shares of the company among several family members, or that they are going to give all shares to one person and make some kind of financial arrangements for the other children. The purpose of the meeting is to find out what they want and to talk about how that fits with what other people in the family want to do.

It is your parents' chance to talk about their vision for their business and your chance to find out how you fit into those plans. Often it will take more than one meeting to hammer out the details of business succession, but in the first meeting you can at least get the general ideas on the table for discussion.

For more information in Canada, see *Succession Planning Kit for Canadian Business,* also published by Self-Counsel Press.

## 6. Maintain Family Harmony

When someone passes away or loses capacity without having done adequate planning, the two areas in which families suffer the most are finances and family harmony. Most parents will say that losing family harmony is worse than losing assets or money. Nobody wants loved ones left behind to suffer for their lack of planning.

The main way that family harmony is disturbed is by having to guess what the deceased or incapacitated person wanted to have done. Each person will offer his or her thoughts or interpretation or belief of what the person "would have wanted" and it is extremely rare that everyone in a family agrees. This is not an abstract or meaningless conversation for most people; it really matters to them to do what a loved one wanted to do. When individual family members are polarized on an issue, it can be impossible to convince anyone that they are wrong.

Almost any topic can be the source of an emotional argument among family members, but some of the most common include:

- Funeral or cremation wishes (almost every detail assumes great importance, including whether to bury or cremate, where to inter, what clothing the deceased should wear, whether the service should be public or private, where to hold the service, whether there is to be a reception, and what should be said in the obituary notice).

- Who is to receive certain personal or household items such as a wedding ring, photo album, or other sentimental items.

- Medical-care decisions, particularly those that may lead to loss of capacity.

- Whether life support should be terminated.

- Whether the person should live in a long-term care facility.

- Which children an aging parent should live with.

- Whether the family home should be sold.

All of these are questions that families aim to answer when holding a meeting. No matter the specific situation, family harmony and understanding your parents' wishes will always be outcomes to try to achieve. Whether other topics need to be covered in your own meeting will depend on your family situation.

# How to Say What Needs to Be Said in a Family Meeting

This chapter looks at how to hold a conversation about estate planning with your parents or other family members. The guidelines in this chapter are about *how* you say things during this important conversation, rather than what you say. See Chapters 9 and 10 for ideas on what to say. The way a message is delivered is very powerful and you should be aware of how your words are delivered.

Given that the topic is already an undesirable one from your listener's point of view, you should do everything you can to put your parents and other family members at ease. Chapter 4, section **4.**, discussed creating a safe environment, which is very applicable to family meetings, so try to apply what you learned to your meeting.

This chapter talks about more than putting people at ease. There are practical ideas

about how to prepare for a meeting, how to run it, and how to handle the people who will be involved. Always keep in mind that what you want to end up with is a legally binding estate plan that everyone can live with. It is a combination of law, business, and extremely personal matters, so it will be unlike almost any other meeting you will ever attend.

## 1. Prepare Ahead

If you are planning to hold a family meeting with several members of your family in attendance, you will find that preparing in advance will make all the difference in whether your meeting runs smoothly. Take the time to think about what you hope to accomplish and what might help you attain that. Even if you plan to hold an informal meeting, you will have to do some preparation to keep it from being a social outing or, worse, a complaints session.

For example, you may be hoping to accomplish the following with the meeting:

- Motivate your parents into making wills and enduring powers of attorney.

- Motivate your parents to start thinking about who will take over the family business.

- Alert your family members to a specific problem or situation that needs to be addressed, such as a parent whose capacity is beginning to deteriorate.

- Find out your family's plans for the cottage, timeshare, or lake lot.

- Find out your family's plans for the family business.

- Come up with a plan to look after an aging person whose health is failing and find out how much time and effort each of your family members is prepared to put into the project.

- Get some input into your own planning.

- Simply make everyone in the family aware of the need for planning.

There are as many different examples as there are families. You need to be clear on why you are holding a meeting and what you think it should be about. Are you aiming for discussion, input, consensus, or simply just listening?

The following are some ideas for preparing ahead for the family meeting. You will have to adapt them according to how formal or informal you think your meeting should be.

## 1.1 Make an agenda

Sometimes people feel that preparing an agenda makes the meeting seem too formal and businesslike. While it is true that the people around the table are family members and not business associates, remember that during this meeting you will be dealing with family business, not recreation. Preparing an agenda conveys the message that the subject matter is important enough to write down and organize and that you expect everyone to give it the appropriate attention.

Making an agenda means writing down a clear list of precisely what you and the others are going to cover in the meeting. Be specific. For example, if your concern is what is going to happen to the family business once your parents are no longer in charge, do not simply put "family business" on the agenda. Make your topic specific, such as "Who would Mom and Dad like to be their successor in the family business?"

You might want to include follow-up questions to round out your topic, such as, "Will all of us who now work at the family business still have some involvement in it once Mom and Dad sell or transfer the business?" Add a number to each topic.

If you think the meeting is going to be quite lengthy, you can put coffee breaks or lunch breaks on the agenda if you wish. Doing this might reduce the number of people who get up and leave the room from time to time during the meeting and possibly miss important things that are being said.

Some people like to put the name of the person who will be talking about a particular subject next to that subject on the agenda. This would be suitable if you are not going to be the only person who brings up a topic, such as would be the case if you will be asking professional advisors to join you.

The agenda serves several purposes. One major use of the agenda is to alert everyone who might be coming to the meeting to what is to be covered. You want to make sure that you give enough information so that each person can identify and understand the topics and can prepare materials or questions if they want to.

You can also use the agenda to estimate how much time is to be allotted for the meeting. You might realize after you list your topics that there is more to be covered than you thought, so a second or third meeting might be needed.

Make sure that your agenda has at the end of it a heading called "New Business." This is the place where anyone coming to the meeting who wants to talk about something not already on the agenda can speak up on the topic of their choice. Everyone will quickly realize that they will be given a fair chance to talk about items important to them and this will help reduce anxiety among family members at the meeting.

Another use of the agenda is to organize the meeting in a logical way so that while you are meeting, you are not jumping all over the place with different topics, wasting time, and confusing people. During the meeting you can check off each item as it is covered so that you can keep track of what is left to be discussed.

To use the agenda, make enough paper copies of it for each person who will be, or might be, attending the meeting. Send out the agenda ahead of time to give everyone a chance to read it. This is a good time to attach anything else that will be talked about at the meeting, such as a doctor's report or an offer to purchase your parents' home.

After everyone has arrived at your meeting but before you start talking about the items on the agenda, ask the group if they have read the agenda. Always ask whether there is anything to be added under New Business. This is the chance for everyone at the meeting to put their own matters forward for discussion, and you should be open to this. If there is anything to be added, write it down under New Business to make sure you do not forget to bring it up.

As you go through the meeting, make sure you follow the agenda as a blueprint. Do your best not to stray onto matters that are not really related to what you are talking about. If people keep bringing up new topics and it will be impossible to cover them all, you may have to schedule another meeting to cover those topics. Even in a small group of only three or four people, following a proper agenda will make you appear serious about the topic, well-prepared, and authoritative.

On the CD that accompanies this book, there is an Agenda Form that you can use for your meetings. It has space for three agenda items and one item of New Business but you can expand it to include as many topics as you like by adding additional rows. You can reuse the form as many times as you need, depending on how many family meetings you decide to hold.

Sample 1 is an example of an agenda prepared using the Agenda Form found on the CD.

## 1.2 Decide who is to lead the meeting

Think about who would be the best person to lead the family meeting. While your automatic response might be that you will lead it yourself, give some thought to family politics. Is there one sibling or other person who is a natural leader among the family? Is there someone who everyone seems to listen to and follow? If there is someone like that, and that person is not you, think about enlisting that person as a co-leader of the meeting. This might bring onside a person who can help control the family group's emotions and reactions during the meeting so that things do not get out of hand.

## SAMPLE 1
# AGENDA

### Date of Meeting: November 15, 2010

| Item | Topic for discussion | Led by | Done |
|------|----------------------|--------|------|
| 1. | Mom and Dad's plans to update their wills to include their grandchildren. In particular, how do the kids feel about setting up trusts to help pay for the grandchildren's education? | Dad | |
| 2. | Who will get Mom's jewelry after she passes away? | Mom | |
| 3. | Mom and Dad would like coexecutors on their wills. Who should be the coexecutors? | Dad | |
| 4. | New Business<br>Will Mom and Dad keep the cottage at Duck Lake now that they are going to retire? | James | |
| 5. | New Business<br>Update on the plans for Mom and Dad's 50th wedding anniversary party. | Noreen | |

A good choice of who should lead the meeting might arise out of the topics themselves. One person might know quite a bit more about the situation than others, making him or her a good candidate to lead the discussion. For example, if one of your siblings has been acting as your parents' representative under their enduring power of attorney for several years and the discussion at the meeting is going to be about finances, that sibling should probably lead the meeting.

Leading the meeting does not mean that you are the only person who gets to speak. It does, however, mean that you enforce the rules about whose turn it is to speak during the meeting.

Perhaps you do not really want to lead the meeting yourself, even though you realize that this is an important meeting for your family. Not everyone is comfortable speaking in front of a group, particularly on emotional or sensitive issues. If you are not going to be able to act as group leader effectively, consider who else you might enlist as a leader. Again, there might be someone among the family members who is a natural leader and who might be much more comfortable in the role than you.

Another choice of meeting leader might be someone in your family who has some training or expertise in the area you are covering. For example, you might have a sibling or cousin who is a lawyer with experience in wills, or a doctor, psychologist, or nurse who has experience with patients with mental incapacity. If the meeting is covering that kind of topic, that sibling or cousin might be the ideal meeting leader.

If you decide that you are going to lead the meeting yourself, you can still call on other family members for help making decisions during the time you are planning your meeting.

Finally, think about whether you are going to need a neutral third party to run the meeting or perhaps attend as backup. Even if you had not originally planned to invite one, you may find that as you tell your family members about the meeting, they begin to argue, become stubborn, or take sides on issues even before the meeting takes place. If you think your meeting is in danger of being nothing but a nasty fight, it is a good idea to hire someone to help you.

The following are some choices for people who can run your meeting for you:

- Family mediators
- Family business advisors
- Family lawyer
- Lawyer who is trained as a mediator
- Minister, pastor, or rabbi
- Social worker
- Family therapist

As you can see, there are options for you if you want or need some assistance. Having a neutral third party at least removes accusations that the person running the meeting is in it for his or her own gain. Sometimes having that stranger in the room causes people to behave better than they might otherwise. Sometimes family members are more willing to take directions or suggestions from someone who is not a family member.

The people who appear on the list are trained in conflict resolution and counseling. They may have more resources to draw on than individuals who do not have that training. Also, they will not have the same level of emotional involvement and will therefore find it easier to remain calm during an upsetting discussion.

## 1.3 Invite the right people

Once you have decided what the meeting will be about and who will be leading it, you must think about who is to be invited to the meeting. It is critical that you invite everyone you need but that you exclude those who do not need to be there. It might be harder than you think to make up your final list of invitees.

If your meeting is going to be about your parents' estate planning, consider whether or not your parents should be present. In most cases, it seems logical that they should be, as one of the main purposes of the meeting will be to find out what they want to do. In some cases, however, it makes less sense to invite your parents even though they might be the topic of the meeting. This is usually a preparatory meeting that takes place before the full meeting. The parents would be present at the full meeting.

Think about whether you would want your parent in the room while you ask your siblings whether or not he or she should be moved into long-term care, or whether your parent's mental capacity has in fact diminished as much as you think it has. You might feel extremely uncomfortable and might not speak your mind out of respect for your parent. Others might be similarly unwilling to state their real opinions because they do not want to upset your parent.

Sometimes meetings are gatherings of the loved ones of a family member who want the chance to confer among themselves first before bringing up something that might prove hurtful to that person. Perhaps you want to decide as a group what your approach to an issue should be, such as regarding a parent who refuses to stop driving even though he or she is posing a serious danger to himself or herself and to those around him or her. Perhaps the group wants to decide which person is able to move homes to be close to a parent who is beginning to show severe signs of deterioration.

The point of a meeting that does not include the parents but that is really about the parents is to find out what support you have on an issue, to find out who is willing to be involved in various solutions, to allocate tasks or decisions among the group, and to show a united, informed front to the parents. Your parents do not want to see you fighting, no matter what your age. The meeting is also to make sure that everyone in the family has all of the latest information needed to make decisions. This kind of meeting is almost always followed by a second meeting in which the family (usually the children of a certain person) tells that person their concerns and the steps they would like to address.

Often children feel guilty having a meeting about parents without the parents present because they feel that they are doing something sneaky or underhanded. If you find the idea bothers you, realize that this kind of meeting can often bring about solidarity among siblings that did not exist before. It can prevent a situation in which several siblings are simultaneously working on solutions, rather than dividing up the tasks between them. Think about how important it is that you and your family members work together to find the best solutions for your parents. Solutions can only be found if all of the facts, even the less pleasant ones, are out in the open and can be talked about.

Once you have settled the issue of whether or not your parents will attend, think about who else should be present. It is all very well to talk about a family meeting but there are several interpretations of who is included in "family." If your meeting is about your parents'

estate planning and your parents are attending, it would make sense to defer to your parents' wishes about who should attend. The subjects being discussed will be legal, financial, and personal, and your parents should be able to decide who is privy to their information.

Your parents will most likely want all of their children present. This, again, seems like a simple sentence but is less so when one or both of your parents have had a previous marriage. While you and your siblings may or may not want your half-siblings from another marriage to attend, the decision is really up to your parents. It is not up to you to influence them either for or against any individual person.

If the children are present, the next question is whether the children's spouses should also be present. This will of course depend on the family dynamics and how close any given individual is with your parents, and again, it is your parents' choice. Most parents state that they do not want their sons-in-law and daughters-in-law to attend this kind of meeting. They feel that the issues to be covered are extremely personal and private and they often state that they want only their own children to be present.

Make sure you cover this particular issue with your parents and then make absolutely certain that your invitation is clear. Tell each of your siblings that in-laws are not included. If necessary, repeat this to the in-laws themselves. Expect at least one in-law to be offended and angry and be prepared to stand your ground. If one of your siblings insists that he or she will not attend without his or her spouse, calmly state that your sibling may stay away if he or she wishes and that you will let him or her know what was decided after the meeting.

If you have a sibling who is estranged from your parents, or who has simply drifted out of everyone's lives over the last several years, find out in advance whether your parents want that person to be present. If the estranged sibling is an adult who is not physically or mentally handicapped, he or she will likely not qualify under the law as a financial dependent of your parent. In such case, if there is no legal requirement to support the person and if there is no personal relationship between that person and your parents, is there really any good reason to invite the person to a family meeting? Having that person in the room might be quite upsetting to your parents.

Most family meetings do not include extended family members such as the siblings, nieces, and nephews of your parents. Whether or not they attend is usually a matter of your parents' choice, but this may be different if there is a family business that is owned or partially owned by people outside of your nuclear family, or that employs extended family members. For example, if your mother and her two sisters are the shareholders of a company, it might make sense for her two sisters to come to a meeting about estate planning to find out how it affects them.

Also consider whether you need or want any professional advisors to attend. If your parents have a lawyer or financial planner that they have worked with for a long time, they may want that person to attend. They might want input or ideas from those advisors, or simply for their advisors to be aware of what is going on. Invite them if this is what your parents want. These advisors are not there to run things, but are present to give expert input if that is needed.

## 1.4 Make sure everyone is clear on the date, time, and place

When you circulate your invitations, make sure that you are clear about when and where the meeting will take place. Choose a method of communication that suits the various people you are inviting. For example, there is little point emailing an invitation to everyone when you know that some individuals do not check their accounts regularly. It may be necessary to use different methods of communication for different individuals:

- Telephone call
- Email message
- Facebook page
- Text message
- Traditional letter
- Greeting card with a note inside
- In-person conversation
- Word of mouth

Prepare the invitation as a separate item then include the agenda in the invitation itself, such as an email attachment. It is up to you whether you ask people to RSVP to your invitation. If you are working with a larger group, you might find it very useful to know how many are attending. With a smaller family group in which invitations are delivered personally, you likely will not have to request responses because they will be given to you automatically during your conversation.

If you are asking a lawyer or advisor to attend, ask him or her to be there a few minutes before the meeting starts so that he or she can be introduced to everyone and circulate any handouts or materials he or she has brought. You will likely find that if you are using a mediator, he or she will want to be present before any of the family members arrive. The mediator is usually only involved if there are volatile issues to be discussed, and will want to head off any arguments that might break out before the meeting even begins. He or she will also want to meet each person who arrives and introduce himself or herself to each person.

Two or three days before the meeting, confirm with everyone that they are still attending.

## 1.5 Prepare the room

Your choice of venue for your meeting will have an effect on how formal your meeting feels to the people who are attending. If you are holding the meeting around your kitchen table, which is certainly acceptable and very common, the meeting will feel less formal than one that is held in a rented hall or someone's office. Many families choose a less formal option because they want everyone to feel at home. It is up to you to decide how formal you want your meeting to appear to others.

Before deciding to hold your meeting at your home, consider what distractions you might have to deal with. Are there children, pets, or others who will demand your attention? Will you have to compete for airspace with a television, stereo, or telephone? If so, perhaps you might hold the meeting at your parents' home or at the home of another family member, where you will have fewer interruptions.

Also consider the seating arrangements. Ideally, the group will sit together at one table where everyone can see everyone else. Everyone should be able to hear each other easily. Chairs should be comfortable; it is not conducive to a productive meeting for people to sit on uncomfortable folding chairs or picnic tables for long periods of time, if that can possibly be avoided.

If you do not have room in your kitchen or dining room, think about how your living room could be modified to hold everyone. Perhaps dining room chairs could be added to the couches and chairs already in the room. Remember that living rooms tend to have less direct light than kitchens or dining rooms and generally do not have enough tables of the right height for people to write on. Consider whether you need a head or front of the room for a leader or mediator to use. Remember to turn off computers, televisions, or other electronics in the living room.

In some cases, a meeting might be held in a rented hall, church basement, local school, or community league not because you want it to feel more formal but simply because the family is a large group. Few family homes have comfortable space for more than a dozen individuals to sit where they can properly hear and see each other, discuss issues, and take notes. If you are worried that your meeting may feel more formal than you intended because of your venue, you might supply coffee or tea or ask some family members to bring homemade cookies or treats. If you are using a rented space, you should also rearrange the furniture into a circle rather than rows, if possible.

Regardless of where your meeting is to be held, make sure that you are there early. Check your room to make sure that you have enough chairs for everyone and that there is good lighting. You might want to supply writing paper and pens. Turn off any television, radio, or stereo. Make some coffee or tea to help everyone relax and feel at home.

## 2. Don't Wait until a Problem Arises

As with most things, it is better to discuss estate planning before you are in the middle of a crisis. It is best to address these questions well ahead of time, if that is possible. When someone is ill or injured, their emotional reaction to talking about topics like dying will be even more pronounced than usual. A person who is beginning to show signs of having Alzheimer's disease will find the issue of losing mental capacity more threatening than he or she would have prior to the onset of the disease.

Because the topic becomes very emotionally volatile and the need to address the immediate illness overshadows the need to plan for its aftermath, try to interest your parents in preparing their documents well before they expect to need them.

Of course planning ahead is good in theory, in real life it does not always happen that way. Do what you can to prevent having to react in a crisis rather than act carefully before there is a crisis. While you may not have a choice in the matter if your parent is already ill, it is a good idea to initiate the estate-planning conversation while everyone is healthy. This will make it a lot easier to maintain a positive atmosphere. It will also give everyone involved more time to think carefully about the various questions and issues that arise.

Mental capacity is needed for a person to sign a will or an enduring power of attorney. When an older person is showing the first signs of mental deterioration, waiting too long can result in the person losing his or her chance to make a will at all. This is one of the main reasons estate planning should be done ahead of time if at all possible.

If you are trying to motivate your parent to act on estate planning and there are no issues at present with capacity or illness, make that a selling point as to why the planning should be undertaken. Be clear about the advantages of planning while everyone is healthy and explain the advantages to your parent. This should make it clear that you do not believe there is a capacity problem and you want to act before there is one, so you should not startle or upset anyone.

For example you could say:

- "We are lucky that you and Dad are still so healthy. Let's take advantage of that and sit down to talk about your estate planning."

Even if the first signs of mental deterioration have manifested — such as occasional memory loss and confusion — it may not be too late for documents to be done. This is not something that you should decide for yourself. You should enlist the help of a medical doctor, preferably your parent's family doctor or a specialist in gerontology. While the decision will not be up to you, you will get to have significant input into the process.

## 3. Admit Your Own Concerns and Fears

As you are the person trying to raise the topic of estate planning with your parents, you must have some concerns about what will happen if the planning is not done. It is alright to state your concerns so that everyone is clear on why you are bringing it up. Everyone has their own reasons, and there is rarely only one reason applicable to a family, but there are some common threads. Depending on your specific situation, you might state one of the following concerns:

- "I'm concerned that my parents might not have set up their assets in a way that will reduce taxes, and there isn't enough money to pay a lot of tax."

- "I'm worried that after my parents have passed away, there won't be a guardian and trustee in place for my handicapped sibling."

- "I'm worried that my siblings and I will fight over assets and personal belongings if there isn't a will that is clear about who gets what."

- "I'm afraid that my elderly parent will be taken advantage of financially unless someone is looking after his or her money."

Also think about yourself for a minute. While estate planning and incapacity planning are about your parents and their needs, they may have more of an impact on you than you realize. Take the time to think about how it feels to be looking after your parents after a lifetime of them looking after you. Not everyone adjusts well to this reversal. The thought of your parents being dependent on you might be frightening or upsetting.

If you find this concept of looking after your parents extremely hard to get used to, you are not alone. It is a huge adjustment. Remember to call on the experts you need, such as doctors, lawyers, and accountants, to deal with your parents' situation, but do not neglect your own needs. Be realistic about what you take upon yourself to accomplish and share the work, where possible, with siblings, friends, or family members. Many people find it useful to join a support group where they can find sympathetic listeners and practical advice.

The stress of adjusting to being the caregiver might be made even worse if you are going through changes in your own life such as retirement or impaired health. Remember that you can burn out with the stress and work of caring for an older parent, so as part of the meeting process make sure that you are calling on all available sources of help and being realistic about what you can accomplish yourself.

It is probably a good idea to voice your concerns during the family meeting, because you will find that others in your family have similar worries. By bringing up your concerns you may trigger a discussion that allows everyone to clear the air.

You might have fears or concerns that sound similar to the following:

- "I'm worried that Mom and Dad will take this meeting the wrong way and end up with hurt feelings."
- "I'm worried that people will pressure Mom and Dad into making decisions that they don't really want to make."
- "I'm worried that this family meeting might be very uncomfortable for everyone."
- "I'm worried that some people aren't going to take this meeting very seriously and that we won't get a lot accomplished."
- "I'm worried that bringing up the subject of money will make me look greedy or calculating."

## 4. Don't Bring up Past Conflicts and Sore Spots Needlessly

In most families, it takes a good deal of thought and tact to keep everyone working together without flare-ups or upsets. Ideally, emotional outbursts should be kept to a minimum because a person who is upset is flooded with emotions that demand attention, and that person is not usually able to cope with the estate-planning process at the same time. You want everyone to be calm and focused and involved in the meeting. Upsetting people will have a negative effect on what you are trying to achieve.

Almost every family has had some history of conflicts between individuals at one time or another. It is a fact of life that some personalities clash with others, even within families. Few families can truthfully say that all of them have always gotten along. Many families also have at least one or two members who have had difficulties with marriages, money, business failures, or addictions. These things happen to everyone as they are simply a part of life, but sometimes they are touchy subjects for the individuals involved and they do not want them discussed in the larger family group.

When individuals do not get along, avoid causing flare-ups between them by affixing blame or criticism. Do not use inflammatory language or refer to incidents that are simply not relevant to the discussion. For example, there is simply no point to saying things like, "You were always worse at managing money than your brother." Try to keep the focus of the discussion on the parents, and behave as if each of you is a team member trying to achieve a common goal. Treat each sibling as automatically being on the team and being an equal player simply by being a family member.

There will be some instances in which the inability to get along is relevant to estate planning. For example, a parent should not appoint two sisters to be coexecutors if those two sisters have repeatedly demonstrated over the years that they simply cannot get along. Remember that all coexecutors' decisions must be jointly made.

Realistically, it is a bad idea to expect ongoing cooperation and harmony from people who do not get along with each other. It is not going to work. Often parents naively believe that forcing siblings to work together will repair the damage done by previous disputes, but that is almost never the way it actually works. Mentioning the friction between them is a good idea if it will change your parents' minds from appointing both of them.

There is a tactful way of dealing with this. Avoid making critical or judgmental statements such as the following:

- "Don't appoint Cindy and Jane together because they'll just fight like they always do and mess up everything."

Try to say something that acknowledges the problem but is not likely to be inflammatory:

- "Both Cindy and Jane would probably feel more comfortable if they didn't have to take on that job together."

Using the less judgmental words removes any blame and will not cause the siblings to feel the need to defend themselves. Go on to make concrete suggestions, such as appointing one sister to be the executor and the other to be the alternate executor who will only act if the first one cannot do it. If you do not know of an alternate solution, it might be a good idea for your parents to visit an estate-planning lawyer who can give them some fresh ideas about executorship.

If there is a personality issue that really does have to be addressed for the purposes of estate planning, then you must treat it in a businesslike, nonjudgmental manner. Otherwise, you risk putting someone on the defensive and derailing the entire conversation. For example, if a family member is one day going to inherit money but has an uncontrolled gambling addiction, it is fair to raise the issue about how that person's inheritance should be looked after. Nobody wants to see the addicted person taken advantage of or in distress.

The key to raising the issue is to do so constructively and show that your concern is for the individual, not for the money. Avoid saying the following things:

- "Your money will have to be held in trust so that you don't blow it."
- "You can't be trusted with money."
- "A fool and his money are soon parted."

- "If you get your hands on this money, it will just disappear in no time."

Try to make a positive statement such as the following:

- "You and your financial future will be better protected if your money is held in trust for you and looked after by someone else."

The point is the same — that the beneficiary needs help handling money — but the delivery of the message is designed to avoid causing embarrassment or anger, and encourage the beneficiary to agree to have his or her share of the estate protected on his or her behalf.

## 5. Be a Good Listener

Going into your meeting, you should have a mindset for listening to what people are going to say. While you may be able to control which topics are placed on the agenda for discussion, you have no control over what people think or say about those topics. Let other people talk, and listen to what they say.

One of the worst things you can do is to appear to everyone present that you are a control freak, which will anger those around you. Sometimes it's a tough balance to achieve; you want to make sure everyone is focused and you want to enforce some rules of behavior, so how do you avoid looking like a control freak? You will be walking a fine line.

One of the things you can do is make sure you ask whether everyone has had a chance to say what they want to say. Write down important points that others make. Do not automatically dismiss their ideas. If someone makes a suggestion that you feel is absolutely ridiculous, follow your own rules about not laughing or bullying. Hear what the person has to say. Ask some questions about how his or her idea

would work or how it would be applied. Ask how the others present feel about the idea.

If you are going to criticize someone who has spoken at the meeting, do so constructively by saying something like the following:

- "I disagree with your idea because ... "
- "I don't think your idea will be easy to work with because ... "

Then give a good reason based on something concrete such as affordability or logistics. Saying "your idea is dumb" or another similar insult is not a good reason.

Decide on how decisions are to be made during the meeting. Decide whether everyone in the meeting will have some input or whether every decision is to be made by your parents (assuming they are the topic of the discussion). If all attendees are to have input, do the decisions have to be unanimous or can they be carried by a majority vote?

If you are the person initiating the discussion, then you should be prepared to act as a sort of chairperson who will control not only what topics are discussed during the conversation but how the individuals behave themselves as well. If you do not, your conversation may not last long enough for anything constructive to be decided.

If the conversation includes a large number of people, for example, your parents and several siblings, you may find it necessary to lay down some rules of conduct at the outset. You do not need to be formal about it or put anything in writing, but you could get everyone's agreement at the beginning, for example, that everyone will take turns and will not talk over each other, or that nobody will raise their voices. Remind everyone that this is just a discussion to see what the ideas and questions are, and that everyone will have a chance to express an opinion.

Controlling the comfort level of the conversation can be nearly impossible when there are a lot of issues to deal with. For example, you may have two siblings who both want to run the family farm after your parents are deceased but the farm is only large enough to sustain one person financially. The debate between the two of them could get quite heated.

If you believe that it is going to be impossible to conduct a reasonable, constructive conversation, consider hiring a family advisor to run the meeting. While this might make things feel a little more formal due to the presence of an outsider, it might help to have a skilled, unbiased third party present to run things. It will prevent you from seeming to take sides.

You can find family advisors by asking for referrals from business consultants, lawyers, and accountants who deal with succession planning for families and businesses. Always find out what the costs will be first and figure out with your family members who will be paying the bill.

Maximize the effectiveness of your meeting by making sure that everyone has devoted their time and attention to it. It is probably better to have this conversation at home or in a quiet restaurant than at a busy, noisy coffee shop, which would be distracting. Ask everyone to turn off their cell phones for a while and to leave small children at home.

If the conversation becomes quite lengthy, and people are getting tired or upset, take breaks for a predetermined amount of time.

Throughout this chapter, we have talked about the need for you to control the ways in which individuals give their comments and suggestions. This is necessary to make sure that there is a constructive conversation with full participation that does not go off track into a brawl or a screaming match. However, you should not be trying to control the content of their messages.

For example, when someone speaks, listen to what he or she has to say. Do not minimize the person's thoughts by telling him or her that he or she is stupid or strange. Ask questions to draw out the person's reasoning or ask him or her to give examples. If you disagree, say so, and explain why, but make sure your reasons are about the point the person made and not about the person himself or herself. In other words, it is fair to say:

- "Your idea for giving the land to the grandchildren might not work because they are too young."

However, it is not fair to say:

- "That was a really dumb idea. What were you thinking?"

Not everyone finds it easy to articulate their thoughts. This is especially true when they are dealing with words and phrases they are not particularly familiar with (e.g., executor, trusts, beneficiaries, power of attorney) and with legal concepts they have never worked with before. Allow them time to explain as best they can without putting words into their mouths. Do not assume you know what other people think about estate-planning issues.

# 6. Take Notes

If you have a conversation or a family meeting about estate planning or incapacity planning, decide whose job it is to take notes (usually called *minutes* when someone records what was said and decided during a meeting). If nobody else volunteers, you will likely have to do this yourself. Use the form Taking Meeting Notes that is on the CD accompanying this book.

The form Taking Meeting Notes can be expanded to be as long as you want it to be. The best use of the form is to print the blank form, take it to the meeting, and write your notes directly on it. You can always add more pages as you need them. If you want to type your notes into the form later, that is an option, especially if your handwriting is messy.

At the top of the form, you will find a place to record the date of the meeting and the name of the person taking notes. Make sure you fill in this information as it will help you stay organized, particularly if there are subsequent meetings. Below that you will see a place to include the names of everyone who was present at the meeting. There is also a place to include anyone who was absent. This refers to people who were invited to the meeting but who either said they would not be there, or simply did not show up. Including them as "absent" is a record of the fact that they were notified about the meeting and chose not to attend.

Below all of this information is the main body of the form. You will see that the body is made up of two columns. There is a wide column on the left and a narrower one on the right-hand side. You will record your notes in the left-hand column. Do not try to write down every word that is spoken, as you will quickly discover that doing so is impossible. As a note-taker, your job is to summarize what has been said in a way that conveys the main ideas of the discussion. You will also record group decisions in this column.

For example, you are taking notes at a family meeting. Your sister, Jaimee, brings up the idea that your mother can no longer live alone. This upsets your mother, who is present, but eventually she agrees to listen to her options. Jaimee asks about the possibility of your mother moving into a long-term care facility. Your other sister, Desiree, suggests that your mother move in with Desiree and her husband. As a group you talk about which option is most workable and affordable. Your mother makes her wishes known, and eventually you all agree that your mother will live with Desiree.

You could not possibly record everyone's statements in this meeting. Summarize what happened as succinctly as you can while still including the important information such as the issue that was discussed and what was decided. In the right-hand column, record the tasks that everyone will do. Sample 2 is an example of what might be recorded on a Taking Meeting Notes form that shows how the above meeting might look.

Remember that in a family meeting, you will most likely cover several topics so your notes could end up being several pages long. As the estate-planning process goes on, the notes might get more and more detailed.

Notes are important because you and your family members are likely to discuss many options and ideas before settling on any given decision. Typically it can be hard to remember exactly what was decided when there has been so much discussion. Tell your parents and other people who participated in the conversation that you will be happy to give them copies of the notes, and then do so.

# TAKING MEETING NOTES

| | |
|---|---|
| Date of meeting: November 25, 2010 | |
| Notes taken by: Francois | |
| Present at meeting: Mom, Francois, Jaimee, Desiree | |
| Absent from meeting: | |

| Topic and discussion | Tasks |
|---|---|
| Jaimee suggested Mom shouldn't live alone for safety reasons. She suggested long-term care but Mom didn't want to live there. It was decided that Mom will move in with Desiree and Jacques. Renovations will be done so that Mom can more easily use her wheelchair. | Francois will list Mom's house for sale.<br><br>Desiree will get estimates on what it will cost to get a wheelchair ramp, grab bars, and to widen the bedroom doorway. |

## 7. Agree to Investigate the Options

As mentioned earlier, you should go into a family meeting with an open mind and listen to what other people have to say. There may be topics raised that you had not expected. Even when a topic is one you suggested, there may be options discussed that you had not considered. You should agree to look into the options that others suggest.

The only way your family as a group is going to find agreement and end up with a legally binding estate plan that pleases everyone is to agree to at least find out whether options are viable.

For example, if you are discussing renovations to your parents' home, and one of your siblings suggests a complete makeover of the downstairs with a built-in walk-in shower and all the latest conveniences, your first reaction might be to believe that your parents cannot afford it. It is, of course, alright to voice your concern that it may be beyond your parents' means, but it is also a good idea to agree to let someone get estimates and find out what exactly it will cost. Everyone has to cooperate in order to shed light on what options are available for your family and what is going to work.

# What Should Be Covered in a Family Meeting: Discovering the Current Situation

The family meeting will be a combination of finding out the current situation and discussing what should be done for the future. These are two distinct steps and you might find that you need two meetings to cover everything. This chapter will be about how to determine your parents' current financial, health, and personal situation so that you can then, as a group, make some plans for the future. It is impossible to plan the next steps if you do not have a clear starting point.

The goal for this first step is to find out the following:

- What assets your parents have, including assets they expect to acquire in the future such as inheritances, proceeds from lawsuits, or insurance policies.

- What legal steps have been taken so far.

- What health and medical concerns are imminent.

- What concerns family members have for your parents' health or assets.

- What, if anything, needs to be done immediately to protect your parents.

On the CD accompanying this book you will find a Family Meeting Checklist. It has space at the top for you to fill in the date of the meeting, which will help you stay organized if you have more than one meeting. You can print off as many copies of the checklist as you need.

The checklist lists all of the items that you will want to mention during your meeting. You will note that there are columns included so that during the meeting you can check off whether each item on the list was "done" or "tabled." By checking an item as done, you are indicating that it was brought up at your meeting. It does not necessarily mean that all steps needed to deal with the item have been taken; it only means that you brought that item up for discussion and things are now under way. By checking an item as tabled, you are indicating that you brought up the topic but the people in the meeting simply decided not to discuss it that particular day. (Tabling something means putting it aside to be looked at another day.)

The person who is taking notes at the meeting should have a copy of the checklist to help keep track of which topics were discussed and which were not. Any decisions made about any of the items (except for tabling) are not written on the checklist; they should be written down in the Minutes and, possibly, on the Task List (more on this form later).

If you wanted to, you could cross out some of the items on the checklist before the meeting takes place, simply to save time talking about items that do not apply to your parents' situation. However, for the first meeting, you probably will not want to remove very many items. You do not want to assume that you know all of the answers to the questions you are asking your parents. The first meeting is a fishing trip to see how much information you can gather.

If you are making a checklist for a second or subsequent meeting, you should be able to look back at the checklist you used during your first meeting, and simply refer to the items that were checked as tabled.

## 1. Set the Ground Rules for the Meeting

Let everyone know that the meeting will be conducted in a businesslike manner. You should lead by example. Insist up front that everyone respect the opinions and ideas of others and that everyone hear each other out.

If the group is quite large, you might have to come up with a way to make sure that people are not talking over each other. This could be as simple as having each person raise a hand until the person chairing the meeting asks the person to speak. While this sounds very formal in the context of a family, sometimes it is the only way to control a large group of individuals.

Advise the group about what will happen if someone leaves before the meeting ends. Most often meetings will carry on and decisions will be made without that person. This prevents any one individual from stopping the meeting if it is not going the way he or she wants it to go. Family meetings can get emotional and it is not unusual for someone to become upset and storm out of the room in an attempt to control what is happening.

It is a good idea to state this rule up front at the beginning of the meeting. If you introduce the rule after a person has declared his or her intention to leave, it appears to be a response to that person in particular rather than a general rule that applies to everyone.

Also talk about how issues are to be resolved. Most commonly, if the meeting is about your parents' estate planning, issues are resolved according to what the parents want. In other words, even if every other person at the meeting disagrees, your parents get to do what they want. This might not be possible if the situation is that your parent is losing capacity and the issues to be talked about are how to deal with that incapacity. While you obviously should not force things on your parent just because he or she is losing capacity, it might be a good idea to have a process in place, and agreed to by all, that what your parent wants might not be the best thing to do.

In Chapter 8, you learned about making an agenda for the meeting. Make sure that everyone has a copy of it before you start, and ask whether there are any items of New Business to be added. If you have any professional advisors at your meeting, people will be wondering what in particular they are there to do, so you should explain their involvement at the time the agenda is distributed.

## 2. Understand the Current Situation

One of the main goals of your meeting should be to understand the current situation. You need to know what is already in place. This involves asking a lot of questions about money, assets, and debts, as well as intentions and desires. In most families this can be hard to get used to as the parents usually do not share that kind of information with the family.

This may trigger a concern about privacy and your parents may object to disclosing their information to everyone. Keep in mind that not everyone needs to know the dollar amounts of your parents' finances, if your parents want to keep that private. Once you have determined the current situation, the discussion will flow into what your parents want to do with their estates once they pass away or lose capacity.

To understand your parents' financial situation, you will need the following information:

- What legal documents are already in place? Some people have wills but do not have incapacity documents. In other cases, you may find that assets have already been placed in a trust. Look for family trusts, bare trusts, executorships, agency documents, etc. Make sure that you are aware of all legal documents that pertain to estate planning and incapacity planning and that you understand how they all fit together.

- Where are their current legal documents kept? If they are in a safe deposit box, where is it? If they are at the lawyer's office, who is the lawyer?

- What life insurance policies are in place? Who are the named beneficiaries? Where are the policies kept?

- Are there any other insurance policies in place, such as long-term care insurance or critical illness insurance? Where are the papers kept?

- Where do your parents bank? Where are their investments? Are the investments in their joint names or in their individual names?

- What pensions are your parents entitled to get? Are there private pensions in addition to any government benefits? At what age will the benefits start and end? Is there a survivor benefit for a parent who is widowed? Is there a death benefit for the estate?

- What beneficiary designations are in place on registered assets?

- Whose names are on the title to the house, cottage, or lake lot? Are the titles set up as joint tenants with right of survivorship, or some other arrangement? If there are joint titles, who are the other people whose names are on title? Are any of the properties in a trust? Where are the deeds kept?

- Are there any trusts in place? If so, who are the beneficiaries? Who is the trustee? What assets are in the trust? Where is the document that sets out the terms?

- Are your parents owners of shares of a corporation and if so, who are the other shareholders and in what percentages?

Is there a shareholders' agreement in place? If so, where is it? Where are the share certificates and minute book kept? Does the company have its own bank account? If so, with which bank?

- What liabilities do your parents have? Are they secured by mortgages or specific assets? Are they life-insured?

- Have your parents signed as guarantors for anybody else's loans?

- Have your parents made any loans to you or other family members?

- Do your parents have assets in other countries?

- Are your parents involved in any lawsuits?

- Are your parents currently acting as executor, trustee, or guardian for anyone? If so, where are the documents that formalize the arrangement? For how long is that arrangement supposed to continue?

- Do your parents give donations to charities or their church?

- Are your parents up to date with income tax return filings and payments?

You will note that these topics are broken down into specific questions on the Family Meeting Checklist included on the CD.

## 3. Who Is Already Involved?

As part of finding out your parents' current situation, you should also find out whom your parents currently rely on for professional help. In some cases you will find that they do not have anyone in a particular profession, which will help you identify which needs will have to be filled in the future.

You should record the names and contact information of the following professionals and caregivers that your parents currently use and want to continue to use:

- Wills lawyer

- Lawyer for other purposes (e.g., lawsuits, corporate matters)

- Banker

- Loan officer

- Mortgage officer

- Financial planner

- Investment advisor

- Insurance broker

- Accountant

- Tax preparer

- Bookkeeper

- Family doctor

- Specialist doctor(s)

- Pharmacist

- Therapist

- Naturopath

- Supplier of specialty items (e.g., wheelchair, oxygen tanks, prosthetics)

- Supplier of in-home providers (e.g., meals, nursing, housecleaning)

- Live-in caregiver

These topics are also listed on the Family Meeting Checklist included on the CD.

## 4. Current Health Concerns

Your parents might be dealing with health or medical problems. In fact, that could be the main impetus behind the current need for a family meeting. Many family meetings happen for the first time in a family as a response to a parent's failing health. If your family meeting is called for this reason, try to get the facts as best you can, including:

- Names and phone numbers of all doctors.

- Names of hospitals or clinics.

- Copies of any reports, X-rays, etc., that your parents are willing to share.

- Name of the condition or illness that is affecting your parent.

- An understanding of the diagnosis and prognosis.

- Date of next appointment.

- Dates and places of upcoming surgeries or treatments.

The most important thing to find out is what help your parent wants at present. Moral support is a given, but try to find out what the current situation demands. Does he or she want someone to drive him or her to and from appointments? Does your parent want help when he or she speaks with the doctor to better understand the options available? Does your parent want someone to stay overnight with him or her in the hospital? Does he or she need someone to pick up prescriptions?

Find out whether there is a health-care directive in place and if so, who the person named as the representative for health-care decisions is. If there is a document in place, find out if there are any specific instructions. For example, some documents state that certain medical procedures such as blood transfusions are never to be used.

# What Should Be Covered in a Family Meeting: Planning for the Future

In this part of your meeting, your goals are to understand what your parents want to have happen with their estates after they pass away, and to understand their wishes in the event that one or both of them should lose capacity to make decisions. Your discussion should touch on retirement, long-term care, and end-of-life decisions. There is a lot to cover when planning for the future so it might take more than one meeting.

The meeting might be shorter if your parents already have solid ideas about what they want, but not everybody has that figured out before the meeting. Your parents, for example, might already have decided that once they are both deceased, their assets will be divided equally among their children. There might have to be some discussion about how, within that general plan, your family could deal with

the cottage or valuable family heirlooms or the car that your dad rebuilt.

Your parents might want to ask you and your siblings whether there are specific items that each of you would like to own. They might need to raise topics such as how to care for a sibling with a disability. You will have to let the topics develop during the meeting as you will not necessarily know in advance how much planning your parents have already done.

In some families, it works best to hold a meeting to consider ideas and discuss them in detail without deciding immediately which way the parents want to go. Your parents, for example, might want to know who is interested in carrying on the family business or who is prepared to be the trustee for a disabled family member. They might ask someone whether he or she would be prepared to be the executor under their wills or their agent under their health-care directives. It is a fact-finding mission for your parents as much as it is for you. Sometimes people want to think things over for a day or two before agreeing to commit themselves to something.

This chapter talks about many of the topics that are often raised in family planning meetings. Reading this chapter may help you to define what your family needs to talk about.

## 1. What Happens when One Parent Dies?

In most cases, a married couple will want to leave everything to the surviving spouse, but it is important that you do not assume this to be the case. In your meeting it should be discussed to make sure that your parents have considered the question, and that the rest of you understand what is to happen.

Often, a parent will want to leave specific items to certain people even when their spouse survives them. For example, women often like to leave wedding and engagement rings to their daughters or daughters-in-law even if their husbands outlive them. You should find out whether your parents want to make any gifts of this kind and if so, whether they want to make that gift while they are alive or whether they want to leave the gift in their will.

The situation may not be simple; for example maybe the parent who dies has been married more than once. In blended families, it is common that the parent will make provisions for the original family as well as the second family. This does not usually include provisions for the first spouse, but it does usually involve some portion of the estate going to the children of the first marriage. Where there is a blended family, it is essential that your parents discuss what they want to do with respect to providing for the earlier family. It is also important that your family members understand that these wishes are to be respected.

Part of this discussion will also touch on who your parent wants to have as his or her executor. Though it is common that the surviving spouse acts as executor of the estate of the spouse who passes away, it is not always what the surviving spouse wants to do. Not all spouses want to take on the work and responsibility of handling the estate, particularly as they get older. They may not want to be in a position where they have to deal with the spouse and children of the first marriage. Even if they do state that they want each other as their first choice of executor, make sure that an alternate is chosen. It is not uncommon that a spouse finds that he or she is simply not able to act as executor because he or she is immobilized by the shock and grief of losing a spouse. If that happens, your family needs to know who the alternate choice is so that person can step in and handle the estate.

## 2. What Happens when Both Parents Have Died?

One of the main discussions you will have during your meeting is what your parents want to do with their estate once both of them have passed away. In fact, this discussion is probably the most detailed and lengthy of all the topics to be covered in your meeting. You will probably find that you will need to consult an estate-planning lawyer if matters are at all complicated, simply because there are a lot of myths and misunderstandings about the law of estates.

The most common arrangement that parents put into their wills for the day when both of them have passed away is a statement that their estates should be divided among their children. It is a simple statement, but putting it into practice can be unbelievably complicated. When the parents express a wish that their estates "go to the children," the following are some of the points that need to be clarified by way of follow-up questions:

- Are all the children supposed to get an equal share?

- If any of the children has borrowed money from the parents, do they have to pay it back or is the loan forgiven?

- If the parents gave a gift of money such as a down payment on a house, does that have to be paid back?

- Do stepchildren get the same share as biological children?

- What do illegitimate children get?

- Do the children of a second marriage get more than children of an earlier marriage?

Aside from the above questions surrounding the inclusion of children, your parents might have other instructions for some or all of the estate. For example, they might want to talk about the following:

- Giving money to charities or a church.

- Giving specific sentimental items such as jewelry to certain people.

- Leaving the house or cottage to one of the children.

- Making financial provisions for the family pet, and stating who should look after the pet.

- Leaving money to grandchildren.

- Leaving money in trust for a disabled relative.

- Putting properties or assets into trusts.

- What to do about a child who is estranged from the family.

- Who will inherit the family business.

- If the family business goes to one child, what the others will get.

Let your parents talk about the plans they have formed so far and let them ask for input if that is what they want from the meeting. It might be that they do not want input but simply want to advise the family of what they are going to do.

## 3. What Happens If One Parent Suffers Incapacity?

The question to be explored here is how to deal with one parent losing capacity while the other may or may not continue to have capacity. If one parent is significantly older than the other, you should accept that the older one is more likely to lose mental capacity than the younger one, but you still have to plan for either one of them to lose capacity.

One of the decisions that has to be made is who will be put in charge of the power of attorney for the person who loses capacity. It is common for a husband and wife to appoint each other as first choice for attorney, though there are situations in which that is not the case. This means that should the husband lose capacity, the wife would have the legal authority to deal with his assets and finances, and vice versa.

They will also need to appoint an alternate person who would act if the first-choice person has passed away or is mentally incapable of acting under the power of attorney or simply does not want to do it. If a widowed person loses capacity and has never appointed anyone but his or her spouse, suddenly that person is left with nobody appointed under the document.

This discussion will eventually turn to finances, as most topics involving estate planning do. If a person is incapacitated to the point that someone has to act under his or her power of attorney, that person is likely no longer earning employment income even if he or she had not yet planned to retire. Because the person is still alive, any life insurance policies he or she may own will not have paid out any proceeds. This means the person may be entirely dependent on savings, investment income, and pensions to cover his or her expenses. This may require lifestyle changes if income is drastically reduced.

Another issue to be covered when one parent becomes incapacitated is whether the incapacitated parent is the one who always handled the family money. It is not unusual in married couples, that one of them is in charge of the household financial affairs (e.g., house title, insurance policies, pensions, and bank accounts), while the other is not involved in those matters more than superficially.

If the parent who becomes incapacitated is the parent who normally handled the finances, the family is going to have to provide more help and put more financial solutions in place than they would if it were the other parent who lost capacity. Every situation needs to be looked at individually with a very practical view as to what works with the individuals in the given situation.

## 4. What Other Living Arrangements Might Have to Be Made?

This question is tied in with the question about a parent losing capacity as well as the questions about how retirement and long-term care are to be funded. It is certainly not unusual for a family meeting to be held to talk about how the family is going to handle the fact that a parent, whether widowed or not, can no longer live at home under present conditions without endangering himself or herself.

Table 1 is taken from "Are Americans Talking with Their Parents About Independent Living?: A 2007 Study Among Boomer Women,[1]" a survey done by the American Association of Retired Persons (AARP) in November, 2007. The survey asked people which of the following living arrangements they had considered for their parents as the parents aged.

As you can see, the replies add up to much more than 100 percent, meaning that individuals are considering different options. This must mean that the answer is not obvious and there are various possibilities open. About 63 percent are considering options that will allow their parent to remain in their own home, with some level of assistance. About 45 percent are considering having their parent move in with them, or another family member. About 41 percent are considering the two options that would see their parent move into one level or another of a facility.

## 5. How Will Long-Term Care Be Funded?

As we cannot predict the future, we do not know who among us will eventually live in long-term care. However, you should proceed as if long-term care is a possibility. Once you make the assumption that long-term care might be required for one or both of the parents, you must think about how that arrangement would be funded. In order to answer this question, your parents will have to divulge the value of their estate so that it can be determined whether they can afford this option.

---

[1]Laura Skufca, "Are Americans Talking with Their Parents About Independent Living: A 2007 Study Among boomer Women," AARP www.aarp.org/research/surveys/livcom/housing/il/articles/boomer_women.html

## TABLE 1
# LIVING ARRANGEMENTS FOR AGING PARENTS

| Proposed arrangement: | Percentage who gave this answer: |
|---|---|
| Your parent moves in with you | 43 |
| Your parent remains in his or her home with paid assistance | 33 |
| A family caregiver moves in with your parent | 30 |
| Parent moves to a facility that offers room, board, and some help with personal care | 24 |
| Parent moves into a nursing home | 17 |
| Parent moves in with another family member | 2 |

Keep in mind that people are usually retired for a number of years prior to going into long-term care so there might not be a lot left from retirement savings to fund long-term care when the need arises. Also unexpected medical emergencies, business losses, market swings, or lawsuits can cause retirement savings to fall below expected levels.

A common solution is that when it is time for parents to go to long-term care, the family home is sold and the proceeds of the sale are used to fund the care. Therefore if your parents own a house with no mortgage that can be sold for a significant price, they might have a built-in source of funding. Keep in mind though that if they do not have any other assets, the house might eventually need to be sold to support the parents in their retirement so it is not always a given that the house can be used to fund long-term care.

Also, selling the family home to pay for long-term care does not work so well if one parent needs to live in long-term care but the other parent is still able to live alone in the house. The bottom line is that in such a case, they are paying for the equivalent of two households; one is the family home and the other is the long-term care facility. Most seniors will find that this will drain their resources quickly. Crunch the numbers at your meeting and if ends do not meet, it might be time to start looking into alternative arrangements such as moving in with one of the children to allow the house to be sold.

Another solution for funding long-term care is to purchase long-term care insurance. It is not the kind of insurance that everyone needs, but depends very much on your financial and family situation. This might be a good idea for someone who does not have a high net worth, or does not have any family members who will provide him or her with a home in the later years. It is worthwhile to discuss this kind of insurance, and its cost, with an insurance representative.

These options might be part of your discussion, as might other ideas for funding long-term care. Assess the options carefully and realistically so that you and your family will be prepared in the event that you are called upon to help pay for your parents' long-term care facility.

## 6. How Will Retirement Be Funded?

Much of the discussion about where and how your parents will live during their retirement will revolve around finances. One of the greatest worries people have about retiring is whether they will have enough money to retire in comfort. Some of the common sources of retirement funding include:

- Savings
- Investments
- Income from family trusts or testamentary trusts
- Public (government) pensions
- Private pensions from employment
- Proceeds of the sale of the family home
- Proceeds of the sale of a business
- Proceeds of a life insurance policy (usually when one parent passes away)
- Long-term care insurance policies

It is a good idea to enlist the services of an experienced financial planner well in advance of your parents' retirement, if possible, to help them calculate how much money they will need to retire and what steps they can take to maximize their retirement funding.

In cases where parents have not been able to accumulate much savings for any reason or do not qualify for any pensions, the children might have to subsidize the parents financially. This is something that could be discussed in a family meeting. If it is clear that some kind of subsidy arrangement needs to be put in place, it is only fair to have all of the person's children present so that they can come to some agreement about what each of them can afford to do.

Another discussion arising from talking about retirement is the disposition of the family business. If your parent (or both of them) has been working for years in a privately owned company, partnership, or sole proprietorship, he or she might want to talk about who will take over the business when he or she retires. This is definitely a conversation that all children of the business owner will want to hear and participate in.

## 7. What Happens If a Child Predeceases a Parent?

In the natural course of events, parents do not outlive their children. However, it does sometimes happen that an accident or illness changes the natural course. When making plans for the distribution of estates after their deaths, your parents should consider what they would want to happen to the share of a child who has predeceased them.

For example, Mr. and Mrs. Williams might make wills in which they state that on their deaths, they want their estate to be divided equally among their three children, Sam, Annette, and Marie. In other words, each of those three children would get a third of the estate after debts and expenses were paid. In the event that Annette passed away before her parents, the will might say that Annette's share is to be divided between Annette's two children. Sam and Marie would each still get a third of the estate. Annette's children would share the third that Annette would have had if she had lived.

This is not the only choice that Annette's parents could have made, or that your parents could make. They could choose to say that if one child dies, his or her share is to be divided among his or her siblings. They could choose that the share goes to a charity. These are less common choices, but are valid just the same. The time to find out that your parents have unusual plans is at the family meeting.

Keep in mind that this kind of decision is not open for negotiation unless your parents specifically ask you and your siblings for input. At this stage of the meeting you should simply be listening to what your parents want, clarifying matters to make sure you understand, and documenting their wishes in preparation for the making of legal documents.

## 8. Succession Planning for the Family Business or Farm

If your parents own a privately held corporation or other interest in a family business, they will have to make plans to sell or transfer the business to someone else, either at the time they plan to retire or at the time they pass away. Ideally the conversation about what to do about the business takes place early enough that your parents have plenty of time to consider options, choose and prepare a successor, or structure a sale in a tax-advantageous way.

There are tax shelters and arrangements available for some methods of handing businesses or farms to the next generation of the family. This is definitely something that will take several consultations with accountants, lawyers, and bankers before it is completed.

In your family meeting, you should listen to your parents' ideas about how they want to deal with their business. On the one hand, they may have firm ideas or wishes, such as keeping the business in the family. They may even have solid ideas about which of the children should carry on the business after they retire. On the other hand, they may want to hear from their children or grandchildren about who is interested in one day running and owning the business.

Typically, there will be some agreement about general ideas for the business, after which it will be necessary for your parents to talk to their accountants or lawyers about how their plans might work. Count on having more than one meeting to resolve all business succession issues.

## 9. Family Trusts

A family trust normally involves parents putting a sum of money into a trust that is set up to benefit a group of family members. The parents can decide which of the family members will be beneficiaries, though the usual arrangement is for children and grandchildren to benefit. Most family trusts are discretionary, meaning there is no set monthly or yearly amount going to beneficiaries. The trustee of the trust (who is named by the parent) has the discretion as to who will get various amounts of money and when they will receive those amounts.

There are various tax advantages to putting money and other assets into this kind of trust, and it is something that is best worked out with an accountant rather than among family members.

## 10. Who Will Be the Executor and/or Attorney?

A vitally important decision for your parents to make is who is going to be put in charge of various legal tasks in the future. In particular they need to decide who is going to be appointed as the following:

- Executor under a will

- Trustee of any trusts created by the will

- Representative under a power of attorney for property and finances

- Representative under a health-care directive

Remember that these documents should appoint both a *primary* representative (i.e., a first choice) and an *alternate* representative. For example, a man making a will might say that his wife is his primary choice and his son is his alternate choice. In most places, it is legally possible to appoint two individuals as *joint* executors or representatives.

The role of an alternate is to take charge only if the primary choice has died, is too ill to act as representative, moves away from the area, or refuses to act as representative. In contrast, when there are joint representatives appointed, they both have to act at the same time and all decisions must be made together. Appointing an alternate or a joint representative helps to make sure that there is no point in time in which the estate is left with nobody in charge.

Your parents may already have a good idea of who they want to put in charge. Whoever they choose, they should ask that person (or people) whether he or she consents to take on that role when the time comes.

## 11. Which Advisors to Use

During your family meeting, you will spend some time finding out the current situation for your parents, both financially and medically. Part of that discovery process is finding out whom your parents currently use as advisors. They will be satisfied with some of their advisors and less satisfied with others. There may be some areas in which they do not have anyone helping them. For example, they may not have an investment advisor or financial planner.

An important part of the meeting is for everyone to agree on who is going to be consulted professionally. One the one hand, this may be an agreement to keep using the people who are currently helping your parents. On the other hand, the family might agree to bring in new people. It is important that everyone know who is involved.

## 12. Tax Implications

Whenever anyone does estate planning, a large part of the conversation will revolve around taxation. The goal is, of course, to keep the tax liability to a minimum so that there are more assets left in the estate for the beneficiaries. This part of the planning process is almost impossible to complete without the input of an accountant or an experienced estate-planning lawyer.

Tax is tricky and many an executor has discovered that the deceased person did not realize that he or she should have consulted an accountant. If you or your parents know an accountant that deals with estate tax planning, it might be a good idea to invite him or her to attend your meeting to give input on the taxation of various plans put forward by family members. Alternatively, if an accountant is not present, you should agree in your family meeting to ask an accountant for an opinion before your parents commit themselves to any particular distribution under the will.

Taxation issues become even more important when your parents —

- own a business,
- want to set up a trust,
- own more than one piece of real estate, or
- own assets in other countries.

## 13. Address the Problem Areas

During your family meeting, you should make sure that unusual or complex issues are specifically addressed so that everyone is aware of the situation and knows what to do. Some of the issues might include:

- There is an incapacitated person in the family who, in the future, might need more money than other family members. For example, one of your siblings might have Down syndrome which prevents him or her from being financially independent, and your parents might be interested in making sure that he or she will be looked after financially. This is something that may be addressed in your parents' wills or in trusts that are specially set up.

- There is a cottage owned by your parents but used by all family members. Your parents might have expressed an interest in keeping the property in the family.

- There is someone in the family who will likely inherit a significant amount of money, which concerns your parents because that person is a spendthrift.

- There is someone in the family who will one day inherit money and who is vulnerable because he or she is addicted to drugs or gambling, and your parents are interested in protecting that person from being taken advantage of.

These are the kinds of issues that, while needing tact to address, should be talked about in a family meeting. For example, if your parents are worried about the Down syndrome child mentioned in the list, they will want to know what kind of support and involvement they can expect from various family members.

## 14. How Will Reporting or Follow-up Be Done?

Before ending your meeting, you as a group should agree on the next steps to be taken, and on when and how others will be advised of the progress. If there is going to be another meeting, it should be scheduled now, even if it is for a tentative date.

Tasks will be assigned to people throughout the meeting. For example, one person might have the responsibility to find a lawyer. Another might be responsible for getting an appraisal on the family cottage. Tasks will be recorded on the Record Tasks from Meeting form provided for you on the CD that accompanies this book. Each task should have a deadline for completion.

As a group, decide how this information will be sent to everyone. For example, if Andrew is going to set up an appointment with a geriatric specialist for an assessment, he will set up the appointment, then report to the person running the meeting. From there, is everyone at the meeting to be advised that the task is finished? Decide whether people get a report each time someone finishes a task, or whether the person running the meeting can prepare a weekly or monthly update to send out to everyone.

Setting up the reporting in advance means that everyone will know who is going to contact them, and when they will be contacted. This means that the person running the meeting will not have to field dozens of inquiries about what is going on.

# What Happens
# after the Meeting?

Hopefully you have now had a successful, useful meeting in which plenty of ideas were discussed and everyone is now motivated to get on with estate planning. You may or may not be planning to have more meetings of this kind.

However, even though your meeting has concluded, your work has not ended. There are still plenty of steps for you to take. In a way, having your meeting with your parents or your family is just the beginning. It is a good idea to take each step following the meeting as quickly as possible so that you keep any momentum going. Motivation is always highest immediately following the meeting so you should capitalize on that. Also, the longer you delay after the meeting has wrapped up, the more people will forget what was actually said and agreed on and the more time you will spend refreshing people's memories.

## 1. Review Meeting Notes

Review the notes that you took during the meeting, or if you were not the note-taker, get the notes from the person who took them and review them for completeness. Check and correct the spelling of names. Also check for blatant errors and fix them. Read the notes to make sure that they fully reflect the decisions that were made during the meeting. The notes are not intended to be a full transcript of every word that was said, but they should contain all of the main ideas and contain a record of decisions that were made.

The notes do not have to be written in full sentences with perfect grammar. They are notes, not an essay. If they are in point form, that is acceptable. However, they do have to be readable not just immediately after the meeting but also weeks or months later after people have forgotten what was said. It is understood that notes are often taken in a hurry and are therefore not very legible. This is the time to tidy them.

The following list includes some things to watch for and correct when reviewing your meeting notes:

- Abbreviations: Common abbreviations such as "etc." are not usually a problem because they are so well known, but watch for other abbreviations that may be misunderstood.

- Initials or nicknames: Make sure you put in proper names so that everyone will know whom you mean.

- Acronyms: Spell out acronyms the first time they are used, followed by the initials in brackets. After that, just use the acronyms. For example, the first time you mention the Land Titles Office, you would describe it as the Land Titles Office (LTO) and then when you mention it again you can just say LTO.

- Words or numbers that are scribbled out with more words or numbers on top (e.g., telephone numbers).

If you recorded your meeting electronically, you will now have to transcribe it, unless all participants in the meeting have access to a computer and are able to listen to an electronic version of it online. If you filmed it, you should make copies for everyone who attended the meeting. Even if the meeting was filmed, you should still prepare a set of written (either on paper or on computer) notes and a list of tasks as outlined in section **2.**

Send a copy of the notes, along with a copy of the list of tasks that people agreed to do (see section **2.**) to —

- each family member who was at the meeting,

- any professional advisors who were at the meeting, and

- anyone who was invited to the meeting but was not able to attend.

Sending an email message with the notes and list of tasks as attachments is perfectly acceptable and will save you time and money.

## 2. Review Tasks

Using the notes taken in the meeting, prepare a list of tasks that individual people agreed to do in the meeting. The Record Tasks from Meeting form is provided on the CD for this purpose. Be as clear as possible about what each task is and what it pertains to. You will find that some people are a bit forgetful or unclear about what they have agreed to do, so you will save time and aggravation by spelling it out for them. It will also remind everyone else what is being done. For example, instead of saying:

- "Francis will check into lawyers."

you can use a more specific entry that will help keep everyone on task, such as:

- "Francis will try to find a lawyer in Mom's part of town who specializes in wills and find out what the cost is for getting a will made."

Every task must have a time deadline attached to it. Hopefully the deadlines were agreed to during the meeting at the time the person agreed to the task, though realistically that does not always happen. There is no point assuming that someone will finish his or her task within two weeks if that person is leaving on vacation the next day. When the list of tasks is prepared, put the deadline in as well. Continuing the example begun above, an even better entry would say:

- "Francis will try to find a lawyer in Mom's part of town who specializes in wills and find out what the cost is for getting a will made, and he will email his results to me within 10 days."

Not everyone will finish his or her task within the time allowed. It is only realistic to expect that life events crowd each other out and everyone has jobs, children, and other matters to look after. However, if you attach a deadline, you increase the chances that the tasks will be completed.

If within 30 days of the meeting you find that only some of the tasks have been done, consider sending a brief follow-up letter to everyone who received notes of the meeting. In the follow-up letter, briefly list which tasks have been completed and thank the people who completed them for being on top of things. Then list the tasks that are not yet done and state that you look forward to getting an update about them. Hopefully this will remind people to get on with the things they agreed to do, and it will also reassure other family members that matters are progressing.

## 3. Set up Appointments

Next it will be time to set up appointments with the professionals that need to be consulted to put the planning into place. The professionals that you need to talk to will depend very much on the specific facts of your situation and no two families will have exactly the same needs. Hopefully you got a good idea in your meeting about who should be consulted in your case.

If the issue at hand is whether one of your parents is beginning to lose capacity, the first appointment might be with a doctor. Most families begin by seeing the parent's family doctor, as they have confidence in that doctor's familiarity with the parent. Also, the parent generally likes to stick with someone he or she knows and trusts. Sometimes the family doctor does a capacity assessment himself or herself, and other times your parent might be referred to a specialist such as a geriatrician (i.e., a doctor who specializes in looking after older adults). Whether or not your parent is referred to a specialist will likely depend on how pronounced any early signs of incapacity might be.

Another appointment that almost all families make during this time is with an estate-planning lawyer. The lawyer will prepare a will, enduring power of attorney, health-care directive, and any other paperwork that is needed for the estate plan that is eventually hammered out. The lawyer will talk through plans, issues, and ideas with your parents to help form the estate plan your parents want.

If you bring the notes you prepared from your family meeting, the lawyer will tell your parents about the legalities of the plans your parents thought of during the meeting. Your parents might discover that there are good legal reasons not to go ahead with some specific aspect of the planning they had thought of, or they might find there is a variation on the plan that makes more legal sense.

The lawyer might recommend that your parents consult an accountant, particularly if there is a possibility of tax implications in the estate plan being suggested, if your parents own property outside of the country they live in, or if your parents own a business.

## 4. Get Documents into Place

Legal documents other than those mentioned in the previous section are sometimes needed too, depending on —

- where the aging person lives (laws vary from place to place);

- the person's marital status;

- if the person has children, stepchildren, and/or illegitimate children;

- the amount of the person's wealth;

- the type of assets the person owns (e.g., real estate, mineral rights, pensions);

- if the person has assets in foreign jurisdictions; and

- any other planning (e.g., family trust) that is already in place.

You will note that all of the documents discussed so far in this section are referred to as planning documents. In other words, they are made before there is any drop in mental capacity or, at worst, when there are early signs of loss of capacity but the aging person is still able to deal with documentation. However, as you may know from your own family situation, not everyone gets the planning documents done in time. If an aging parent does not make planning documents while he or she is mentally healthy, the chance to do so is lost.

If this happens to your parents, you may find that not only are there no planning documents, but there will never be any planning documents due to the lack of mental capacity. You cannot allow someone to sign a document when he or she simply does not understand it or know why it is being signed. In such a case, there is an alternative. The alternative is more expensive, time-consuming, and invasive than preparing an enduring power of attorney or health-care directive, but it may be your only option. The alternative is being appointed by the court as a legal trustee of your aging parent's money and property while the parent is still alive.

Though much of the focus of this book is about talking to your parents with a view to having their estate planning put into place, it might be a very good idea to use the opportunity to have your own planning completed as well.

## 5. Do Necessary Research or Get Documentation

At this point your parents need to gather the information that is needed for them to attend the appointments that have been set up with the advisors. They will likely need the following information:

- Bank statements

- Investment statements

- Property deeds (e.g., for home, cottage, investment properties, mineral rights)

- Any recent appraisals on real estate

- Medical reports

- Divorce decree or death certificate (if either of your parents had been married before)

- Social Security Number (United States) or Social Insurance Number (Canada)

- Last year's income tax return

- Incorporation papers (if they own a business)

## 6. Put Some Solutions into Place

In Chapter 12, you will find descriptions of several financial and nonfinancial steps that can be taken by you or your parents during the estate-planning process. They are referred to as "solutions" because they are answers to the questions you and your parents will be talking about in your family meeting.

Each solution presented is described thoroughly enough that you should be able to gain a general idea about it. Some solutions you will be able to see immediately are not going to suit you and your family, while others will pique your interest. Once you see some that interest you, you can raise them at your family meeting as a possible solution to various situations and have your family members discuss them to see what fits. You can also research them or talk to your lawyer or accountant about them.

Once you have held your meeting and have consulted with the professionals you need to see, it is time to get some of the solutions in place. At this stage either you or your parents (depending on capacity) will be giving instructions to the lawyer, accountant, or other individuals to get matters underway. There will be a flurry of activity that might include documents being signed, money changing hands, or titles being transferred.

## 7. Have a Follow-up Meeting or Report to the Group

During your meeting you would have discussed how and when your family members were to be kept up-to-date on developments. Assuming you did that, you will know whether you should be holding another meeting, writing to them, etc. Once all of the estate-planning steps have been taken, you should send around one last communication to everyone to let them know that the plans your parents wanted have now been implemented.

# Possible Financial Solutions That Might Be Discussed at Your Family Meeting

In this chapter and Chapter 13, you will find several ideas for solutions to the issues you have raised or identified through your family meetings. Some of these you can implement yourself, though most will require help from a lawyer, an accountant, or a banker. It is always a good idea to talk over general legal information with a lawyer to make sure you know how it applies to your situation.

The idea is to look at your parents' situation and identify as clearly as possible the issues and problems that need to be resolved both in the present and in the future. As every individual is unique, so are his or her needs. As our parents age, some will experience memory loss and some will not. Some will encounter physical limitations and some will not. Try to evaluate your parents' situation realistically and not have preconceived ideas about what you think they might need.

As you go through the ideas and solutions presented here, remember that some of them will be exactly what you need and others will not be relevant at all. Pick out those that would appear to be useful, then put them on the agenda for your family meeting. Note that there is not only one solution that is right for any one person; most estate plans are a combination of financial and nonfinancial solutions.

Once you have agreed in your family meeting that a particular solution seems like a good idea for your family, follow up with a lawyer, an accountant, or other relevant people to see whether the solution can be implemented.

Whether or not any given solution works for you and your parents will depend on the following:

- Their specific needs. (Are their limitations physical or mental, or both?)

- The type and extent of help your parents are willing to accept.

- Whether any legal documents granting legal authority of any kind are already in place.

- The cost of the solution and your parents' ability to pay those costs.

- The geographic availability of people or institutions (e.g., lawyers, hospitals, doctors, accountants, caregivers) that you need.

- The availability of other family members to assist you.

In this chapter you will find financial solutions to the issues or concerns raised in your meeting, and in Chapter 13 you will find nonfinancial solutions. The financial solutions relate to issues that involve money and/or property. For example, in your family meeting you might have talked about how to make sure that your aging father has help with the banking. A solution to that might be a power of attorney that allows one of the children to do the banking.

The nonfinancial solutions are those that relate to personal or health-care decisions. For example, in your family meeting you might have discussed whether your widowed mother is going to be able to continue to live in the family home or whether she will have to move to a long-term care facility. A solution to the issue might be to arrange for live-in help for your mother.

The solutions discussed in this book are not mutually exclusive. In fact, for most people, a family planning meeting in which several issues are discussed will result in several solutions being put into place together. Therefore you should take note of all solutions that might seem relevant to your family.

In this chapter, the various solutions are defined briefly in order to give you ideas about what is available generally, and how each solution might fit into an estate plan for your parents or your family. There is much more to be said on every one of these solutions, but it is beyond the scope of this book to fully discuss all of them. The definitions provided will give you an idea about whether you want to know more about each solution. If you think they might work for you, make a note to ask your estate-planning lawyer for more information.

## 1. Assets in Joint Names

Most people are familiar with certain joint assets, such as bank accounts. In this kind of account, the money in the account legally belongs to both people, even if only one person is putting money in the account. The word "joint" in this context refers not only to having more than one name on a bank account; it also refers to the legal *right of survivorship*. When one joint owner dies, the other joint owner automatically owns the entire bank account. In fact any asset, whether it is a bank account, residence, or any other asset that is held in joint names gives rise to the right of survivorship.

Joint ownership is usually the way that a married couple owns their family home, cottage, and savings. They set things up this way so that when one spouse dies, the other one can carry on with the least amount of delay, paperwork, and expense. It is a way for spouses to protect the family unit.

Joint ownership is not always well understood, even by people who have property that is jointly held. Most people do not realize that it is possible to have more than one name on a title without that title being joint. For example, title to a house can be held 20 percent by one person and 80 percent by another. There is no right of survivorship there.

One of the reasons families like to use joint ownership of assets is to avoid the probate process. Joint assets with a right of survivorship are not part of your estate and therefore are not included in probate. Keeping assets out of probate holds down costs and time spent on paperwork. However, do not assume that this will work for you; check it with a lawyer before going ahead. Many families have found after the fact that although they avoided probate, they created a whole new set of problems to deal with.

One of the reasons you need to talk this over with a lawyer is to make sure that you and your parents understand the tax consequences of transferring property into joint names. Will the tax bill be so large that it is actually less expensive to go ahead with probate? At what stage of the transaction will the taxes arise? Who will pay the taxes? If the taxes are to be paid from the estate, is there enough money in the estate to pay them? All of these questions and more need to be answered by an experienced lawyer or accountant.

You need to know what rights are being gained and lost on both sides. Most importantly, you need to know whether changing the title is really going to accomplish what you think it will accomplish. With legal strategies, you should always get legal advice about your idea before going ahead, or you might end up spending time and money to try to unwind what you have done.

The use of joint names on assets in estate planning is so common, and so badly done a lot of the time, that the cases end up in court. One of the biggest problems is that after the parents pass away, the child whose name is on the title then owns the asset. The other family members expect that child to divide the asset among them, and sometimes that happens. In many cases however, the child states that the parents wanted him or her to keep the property for himself or herself. As the parents are no longer around to clear up the question, it falls to the court to decide whether or not the child gets to keep the asset.

In some cases, the court is making the child pay back the asset, and in other cases it does the opposite. That is just one more reason to get legal help with any estate planning that might involve putting your parents' assets into joint names with someone else.

## 2. Bare Trusts

A bare trust, which goes by other names as well, is a very simple document that is intended to clarify ownership of assets. It is often used in estate planning or with incapacity issues when a parent puts an asset in joint names with an adult child. This is important because the family members need to know whether putting that asset in joint names was done so that the child would inherit the asset when the parent passed away, or whether it was put in joint names just so that the child could help the parent. A power of attorney is likely the best way to deal with this situation, but a bare trust is an alternative that is available.

The most common example of a bare trust can be used with joint bank accounts. Often a parent will put a child's name on his or her bank account simply for convenience; the parent wants help with the banking. In that situation, the parent does not intend for the child to own the money after the parent dies. In fact, many parents, when this issue is brought up, will say something like "I trust my son or daughter to do the right thing and split the money with the other children." Unfortunately, things do not often run as smoothly as planned. It is not always messy because the child is greedy, though that is occasionally the case; often it is a matter of the child believing the parent intended him or her to own the asset.

Once the parent has passed away, the children have to figure out and agree on what the parent intended. Keep in mind that after a death in the family, the children will be emotional and upset, and not at their best. Decisions and agreements that might easily be made when everyone is calm and happy become nightmares when everyone is upset. A bare trust allows the parent and child to sign a simple document that basically states that the child's name is only on the account for convenience and when the parent dies the proceeds of the account are to fall into the parent's estate for distribution under his or her will. The bare trust clarifies the situation so that arguments are prevented.

## 3. Wills

Most people are at least somewhat familiar with wills, though a will can do much more than most people realize. The main goals of a will are to —

- put a named person (the executor) in charge of a person's affairs upon his or her death,

- name a guardian for minor children,

- direct where the person wants his or her assets to go after his or her death,

- ensure that the person's executor has the legal authority needed for his or her estate to run smoothly, and

- avoid financial losses and emotional disputes among family members after the person's death.

In your family meeting or your discussion with your parents, you will almost certainly ask whether your parent has a will in place. Take that discussion further and ask when the will was last reviewed by a lawyer. Although a will does not expire, it can be badly out of date if your parent's life has changed since the will was made. Your parent might want to review and possibly update his or her will if —

- the person named as executor has died, lost mental capacity, or moved out of the country;

- your parent has been widowed;

- the beneficiaries named in the will have died;

- a beneficiary named in the will has an addiction, a pending divorce, or some other reason for his or her share to be held in trust;

- there are more beneficiaries that your parent would like to include, such as grandchildren or great-grandchildren;

- your parent has remarried since the will was made;

- your parent has become estranged from one of his or her children;

- your parent's financial status has changed dramatically, either for the better or for the worse, since the will was made;

- your parent has bought property in another country;

- your parent wants to plan to avoid taxes as much as possible;

- your parent wants to set up a trust for grandchildren; or

- your parent is interested in donating money to charities in his or her will.

The biggest issue for seniors who want to make new wills is incapacity. Everyone who makes a will must have the mental capacity to understand the effect of the decisions he or she is making. For some seniors, this becomes a problem because they are experiencing the onset of incapacity, particularly memory loss. If incapacity is advanced, your parent will not be able to make a new will. A great deal of care is usually taken by wills lawyers, doctors, social workers, and anyone else involved with a senior that the senior truly does understand what he or she is signing and is signing it voluntarily.

## 4. Enduring Power of Attorney

A power of attorney is a legal document in which one person gives another person the legal power to act on his or her behalf. A power of attorney that is described as *enduring, continuing,* or *durable* is a specialized kind of document that is used in estate planning. Though wording varies from place to place, the legal concept is the same. Its unique characteristic is that it "endures" through mental incapacity of the person who signed it. In other words, if you sign an enduring power of attorney while you are mentally healthy and you later lose your mental capacity, your legal document is still valid.

These documents were specially designed for estate planning and incapacity planning because they give people the chance to choose someone to speak for them and make decisions for them in the future when they need the help.

Enduring powers of attorney are broken down into two categories. One is *immediate* and the other is *springing* (the word springing might be replaced by a similar word depending on where you live). These two categories refer to when the document comes into effect.

The most popular form of enduring power of attorney for estate planning purposes is the springing document. The key to this document is that a person signs it while he or she is mentally healthy and the document is not used until that person loses his or her mental capacity. When that happens, the document is sprung into effect by having a doctor (or two doctors) sign a declaration that the person has lost capacity.

An immediate power of attorney, as you might anticipate from the name, comes into effect immediately upon its being signed. This means that whomever you name as your representative under the document has legal authority to start dealing with your assets as soon as your signature is on the paper.

Though an immediate enduring power of attorney is not nearly as common as the springing enduring power of attorney, there is a particular niche of people for whom the immediate document is the perfect solution. They are individuals who can anticipate that they are about to experience loss of capacity for some reason. For example, a person who is going to have major surgery which is risky and involves a lengthy recovery time or the use of strong painkillers might want to put someone else in charge of financial matters right before he or she goes in for the surgery.

The immediate enduring power of attorney is also used where an older parent is beginning to notice the early stages of Alzheimer's disease or dementia. Rather than go through the process of medical evaluations to determine whether he or she has enough mental capacity to carry on looking after his or her own affairs, the person decides to bypass all of that and put the document into effect right away. If the early signs of Alzheimer's disease are present, it is essential that the document be signed quickly, before the disease progresses to the point where capacity is lost.

With an immediate enduring power of attorney there is no need for any doctors to sign certificates saying that the person does not have capacity. This might allow the aging person to maintain a little more dignity.

## 5. *Inter Vivos* Trusts

An *inter vivos* trust is one that is set up by a living person, as opposed to a trust that is set up by a will after the person dies. The person who owns the assets (often called a *donor*) puts them in the hands of a trustee, who holds on to the assets during the donor's lifetime and after it as well. The donor decides who is to get the assets after he or she dies, known as the *beneficiaries* of the trust. After the donor dies, the trustee transfers ownership of the property to the beneficiaries in the way described by the donor in the trust deed. This kind of trust is usually *revocable*, meaning that the donor can change his or her mind during his or her lifetime and take the assets back out of the trust.

It is very rare that a client requests his or her lawyer or accountant to set up this kind of trust, as most people are not particularly familiar with trusts. It is almost always the other way around — the lawyer or accountant suggest an *inter vivos* trust as a solution to a specific issue or problem he or she encounters during estate-planning discussions.

## 6. Custodial Types of Accounts

There are a dozen variations on these accounts, but in general this heading refers to accounts at banks or trust companies that are managed on behalf of your parent. All of the usual automated debits and credits can be run through the account. The difference is that with a custodial account, the bank or trust company will also take care of other financial transactions, such as getting your parent's tax return prepared, investing any overage in funds, managing investments, paying bills, and notifying your parent when a financial instrument matures and needs to be reinvested.

This can be a useful solution for a parent who does not handle money well or does not want to handle finances. Sometimes this is because of the onset of mild memory loss due to aging, but it can also be quite useful for someone who has perfect mental faculties but does not want to take care of those matters himself or herself. This sometimes arises when a parent is widowed, and the spouse who passed away was the one who always handled the family's money. The surviving spouse may find it stressful or even overwhelming to try to learn how to handle the finances.

## 7. Court-Appointed Trustee

The courts may appoint a trustee for an adult who is not capable of looking after his or her own financial affairs. This can apply to aging parents if they are beginning to lose their capacity due to any one of several dementias or other issues. A trustee is anyone who handles money, or documents, for the benefit of another person.

This solution is appropriate when your parent has not made an enduring power of attorney naming someone to act on financial decisions and has lost capacity to make this document. Usually if there is a valid power of attorney in place there is no need to have a trustee appointed, because a court-appointed trustee does basically the same job as an attorney under power of attorney.

Note that putting a court-appointed trustee in place is only appropriate if your parent has lost mental capacity to the point at which he or she cannot make financial decisions anymore and cannot deal with legal documents in order to appoint someone himself or herself. Incapacity is key to this arrangement as the court is not going to appoint a trustee for an adult who is capable of looking after his or her own affairs.

In order for the courts to appoint a trustee, someone must step forward and offer to take on the position. This is something that you and your family members might discuss among yourselves if you believe this to be an appropriate solution for your parent. You will also need someone to agree to be an alternate trustee who will act if the first trustee passes away, moves far away, becomes ill, or for any reason can no longer continue on in the role of trustee.

If you are considering taking on the role of trustee for your parent, it might be a good idea to consult a lawyer first, or to read as much applicable material as you can before you agree. You should understand that there can be personal liability for you if you should fraudulently or negligently cause a financial loss to the assets you are looking after (note that you will not be held responsible for things beyond your control, like a global stock market crash).

Also make sure that you fully understand the limits of what you can do as a trustee, as this is an area in which a lot of well-intentioned trustees make mistakes that land them in legal hot water.

In Canada, look for *Protect Your Elderly Parents: Become Your Parents' Guardian or Trustee*, also published by Self-Counsel Press.

## 8. Written Business Succession Plan

If your parents own a business, they should seriously consider putting the plans they set up for the future of their business into writing. The fact that this agreement is written down is absolutely key. It is not enough to agree verbally. This agreement should cover the following:

- Who (i.e., family and nonfamily) is to take on various roles and responsibilities within the business after your parents leave (e.g., president, shareholder, director, manager, employee)?

- What will be the extent and nature of your parents' involvement and/or authority after they leave? Will they be consultants? If so, for how long? How many hours will they put in or what kind of projects will they be involved with? How will they be compensated? Will they keep any ownership in the company?

- Who will own shares of the company?

- Who will have voting control of the company?

- How will disputes among family members be resolved?

- How will the rules or structure be changed when they need to be changed?

- How much information is to be given to family members and in what form (e.g., annual report, family meetings)?

- How are changes such as death, divorce, and incapacity of shareholders, directors, and management going to be dealt with?

- How much income or pension will your parents receive from the company after they leave?

- How much will they be paid, if at all, for their shares of the business when they transfer it to their *successor* (the person who will run the business after your parents retire or sell)?

## 9. Selling the Business

During your meeting with your parents or your family, it might have become clear that your parent needs or wants to sell his or her business at some point. If your parent is showing early signs of dementia or incapacity, the sale might need to happen fairly quickly. If mental health is not an issue, your parent may have plenty of time to look around for an opportunity to sell the business in the future.

Assuming that one day the business will be sold, your parent will have to make some big decisions about the general direction of the sale. For example, the buyer could be one of the following:

- A family member, usually of the next generation after your parent's generation. If your parent does not know which particular child within the family might one day own the business, he or she should still form a general idea of whether or not he or she plans to keep it within the family. A family meeting is an excellent place for your parent to talk about his or her wishes and plans for the future and for all family members to find out who among them is interested in taking over one day.

- A group of managers or key employees. If this kind of buyout is being anticipated, it often means that your parent is going to be bought out over time, with payments coming on a regular basis from the future profits of the business. If your parent is considering this kind of arrangement, he or she should consult an accountant to talk about tax implications, and a lawyer about the written agreement that must be put into place.

- An independent, nonfamily purchaser.

If your parents are considering any one or more of these sale options, they will find that they will likely need several meetings to solidify the plans.

Plenty of family meetings are held to talk about what to do with family businesses in the future, even when the parents are not experiencing any symptoms of mental or physical deterioration. In fact, advisors such as lawyers and accountants continually urge business owners to have this kind of meeting well in advance of any projected retirement or sale date. The earlier the business owner gets started on planning, the more options he or she has to choose from.

In Canada, look for *Succession Planning Kit for Canadian Business,* also published by Self-Counsel Press.

## 10. Informal Trusteeship

The word "informal" is used here to differentiate this from the process of appointing someone as a trustee by the court. A court-appointed representative would be a "formal" trustee. An informal trustee is not appointed by the court but is put into a position of trust for a parent by someone who has a financial obligation to the parent.

For example, your parent might be receiving a government pension based on his or her age or military service record. Perhaps your parent cannot look after his or her own money well any more and needs help receiving the pension benefit and paying the bills with it. If the pension is the only monetary asset that your parent owns, it would not be economically feasible to spend a lot of money on having yourself appointed by the court as a trustee. You might even spend more in fees than your parent actually receives in pension benefits.

In a case like this, you can sometimes arrange with the pension plan itself for you to be put on record as the trustee for your parent. This would allow you to receive the pension, deposit it into your parent's bank account, and then use that bank account to pay your parent's bills such as electricity or rent. Having this authority would not give you any access to other assets your parent might own, such as a house or an inheritance from a relative's estate.

You can look into this option for many government plans that pay benefits for retirement, service, or disability, and many private plans as well.

This solution is best suited to parents who receive a pension benefit but do not have other assets that need to be managed or disposed of at the present time. If at some future time a formal trustee is appointed by the courts, it will override any and all informal trusteeships.

## 11. Beneficiary Designation

When you buy a life insurance policy, you will be asked who should receive the proceeds of the policy on your death. Similarly, if you own certain registered financial products such as registered retirement savings plans, you will be asked who should receive the proceeds of those products on your death. The person who will receive the proceeds when you pass away is referred to as a *beneficiary* of the proceeds. When you name the person on your policy or plan, you are *designating* a beneficiary.

Beneficiary designations can have a huge impact on estate planning. When you designate a beneficiary, the proceeds do not become part of your estate, and are therefore not controlled by your will. When you pass away, the beneficiary is paid directly by the insurance company or the bank without any involvement of your will or your executor. Accordingly, when you are deciding what to do with "your estate" in your will, you must realize that you should not be including any policy or product that has a designated beneficiary.

An exception to that general rule is that if the beneficiary you have named is your estate, then it is governed by your will like everything else you own. Also, if the person you have named as beneficiary has already passed away, the money will become part of your estate. For example, if a husband names his wife as the beneficiary of his life insurance policy but she dies before he does, then on the husband's death, the insurance money will be paid into his estate.

You can use a beneficiary designation to create new cash flow in your estate, if you use it correctly. For example, if you are concerned about how your estate will pay taxes on your death, you might decide to buy a life insurance policy that names your estate as the beneficiary. Then, on your death, the policy pays your estate and the money can be used to pay taxes.

Beneficiary designations can be tricky and there are tax implications for financial products. Be careful about setting these up on your own for your parents without finding out how they will affect your parents, their beneficiaries, their taxes, and their estate. If you are interested in talking about how they can help in your case, you should talk to an estate-planning lawyer or a certified financial planner.

# Possible Nonfinancial Solutions That Might Be Discussed at Your Family Meeting

The following are brief descriptions of some of the options that may be available to your parents or family members. These are all options that are not directly related to finances; they deal with personal, household, and health-care matters. This covers a surprisingly large variety of issues, some of which include:

- Where a parent will live.

- With whom a parent may live.

- Nutrition and hygiene for the parent.

- Health care, medications, and treatments the parent will receive.

- Which doctors, therapists, and specialists may treat the parent.

- What social activities the parent may become involved in.

- Whether the parent may work, either for pay or as a volunteer.

- Whether the parent may continue to drive a vehicle.

- Whether life support should be discontinued.

As you can see, these are important, personal issues that will affect your parent every day. You must take the responsibility seriously when you begin to become involved in these decisions on behalf of your parent. When you and your family are discussing these options, keep in mind that you are looking for the solution, or combination of solutions, that fit your individual parent. The fact that something was suitable for someone else does not mean that it is suitable for your parent.

It is essential that you only look for solutions to problems that actually exist. If the only change your parent needs to make is to quit driving, for example, then do not overextend your help to move him or her to a long-term care facility. Take the time in the meeting to truly understand what is needed, then find the appropriate solution that is neither too heavy-handed nor inadequate.

If you are looking at this list of solutions, you are quite likely worried that your parent is experiencing some memory loss, confusion, or other indication that his or her mental capacity is diminishing. Try not to think of mental capacity as being either 100 percent there or 100 percent gone. You have to realize that even when the early stages of incapacity have begun, your parent may be able to live relatively independently for some time. The decline of mental capacity may take many years, and you do not want to impose an unduly restrictive solution on your parent. Try less intrusive solutions before trying those that will take away much of your parent's independence. As you read the various solutions proposed here, think about whether each one would work for your parent, particularly when combined with one or more of the financial solutions mentioned in Chapter 12.

The idea here is to familiarize you with the various documents and solutions that are available so that you can put together a preliminary plan before you go to see an estate-planning lawyer. By doing this, you can form a rough idea of what you want to do, discuss it with your family members, and find out who is willing to take on the various roles and responsibilities.

## 1. Health-Care Directive

Note that a health-care directive may also be called a health-care proxy, advance health directive, personal directive, or living will, depending on where you live.

A health-care directive is a legal document that names someone to make health-care and personal decisions for another person. It is most commonly used when someone is admitted to a hospital or long-term care facility. If the person who is having a health crisis cannot speak for himself or herself, the health-care directive names someone who can step in and speak for him or her. For example, if the person were in a coma or was extremely confused, the person named in the health-care directive would speak to the doctors and give the necessary permissions for tests, medications, surgery, or treatment to proceed.

This kind of document is made ahead of time while the person signing it is still healthy. It is made in advance to be ready when an emergency happens. Most people make a health-care directive at the same time they make their wills. One of the main reasons people like to make a health-care directive is that it prevents a situation in which the family members are fighting about what medical procedures their parent should have, and the doctors do not know who to listen to.

A health-care directive can address specific treatments. For example, if the person making the health-care directive knows that he or she has cancer, he or she can give instructions about chemotherapy, surgery, or radiation. More commonly, though, the documents are made to be very general since we do not know what is going to afflict us in the future.

The documents usually address a person's wishes for end-of-life decisions such as whether or not to take a person off life support if he or she is being kept alive artificially. It is impossible to exaggerate how important it is to have this addressed ahead of time by the person whose life is being prolonged. If a person does not address it, the children may be forced into a situation in which they are being asked to decide whether or not the person is to be kept alive artificially. This is one of the most emotional decisions a parent could possibly ask his or her children to make and it is not at all unusual for children to disagree with each other about what the person would have wanted. Putting it into a document relieves them of having to decide that for the parent and therefore preempts a lot of fighting.

## 2. Court-Appointed Guardian

Normally a guardian is only appointed by the courts for an adult if that adult loses capacity and has not put his or her own documents (e.g., health-care directive) in place. The legal procedure of appointing a guardian for an adult is intended to be a backup for those who did not or could not plan ahead for their own incapacity. The idea is to ensure that an adult who is losing the ability to make reasonable decisions for himself or herself has someone who can help with those decisions.

This book uses the word "guardian" as separate from "trustee" although in some states and provinces the words are used interchangeably. In this section of the book we are talking about nonfinancial decisions so the word "guardian" is used to refer to someone who is making personal decisions for the adult.

The process, costs, and time investment to have someone appointed by the court vary widely from one region to another, but the underlying principles are the same everywhere. Those principles are that an adult has lost the ability to make reasonable decisions for himself or herself and needs the help of another person to make financial decisions, or personal and health decisions, or both.

In most jurisdictions, the appointment of a guardian is considered to be a pretty invasive

step, as it is not something that the individual in question asked for or has control over. It is something that is initiated and controlled by other people on behalf of the incapacitated individual. In many places, the guardianship order is also very comprehensive in that it gives the guardian an extraordinary amount of legal control over another person.

For example, the guardian can decide where the aging parent is going to live, which doctors he or she will consult, and which medications he or she will take. The level of daily control that can, at times, be exerted over another person can make the guardianship order very invasive, particularly if the guardian is heavy-handed. Because of this, guardianship should only be used as a last resort in cases where the parent has done no planning and documented no choices or wishes.

Guardianship is also used when there is a dispute among a person's children as to who is entitled to make decisions, or where one is challenging the decisions made by another. It is a sad fact of life that children of aging parents do sometimes get into bitter disputes over matters relating to their parents. If things cannot be agreed on by negotiation or mediation, they will have to be decided by the courts. If the court wants to put a particular person or combination of people in charge, this will generally be accomplished in the form of a guardianship.

If your family discussions about looking after your parents continually break down into irreconcilable fights, you may end up consulting lawyers about getting a guardianship put into place. Hopefully it will not go that far, as it can be impossible for families to maintain their relationships with each other once they have fought over something so important in court.

This is not to say that guardianships are *only* used where there are disputes, because that is not the case. In fact, the vast majority are put into place with no objection by anyone, as the families agree that the person making the guardianship proposal should be the guardian.

The process of having a guardian appointed always involves getting medical evidence that the aging person has in fact lost the ability to make decisions. Legally, adults are assumed to be competent to look after themselves unless it is proven otherwise, so this medical evidence is essential to justify bringing a guardianship application before the courts.

One of the main advantages of having someone appointed as guardian for an aging parent is that it puts someone in charge. There is no longer general chaos or confusion about who is supposed to be making arrangements, calls, or decisions on behalf of the parent. In some families there are too many individuals trying to make these decisions and in other families there are not nearly enough, but in both cases it needs to be clear who has legal responsibility for looking after the parent. It gives certainty and predictability not only to the family members but to the parent himself or herself, who will know who to go to with concerns or ideas.

In Canada, look for *Protect Your Elderly Parents: Become Your Parents' Guardian or Trustee*, also published by Self-Counsel Press. This book gives step-by-step instructions on how to make applications to the court to be appointed as a guardian. It also gives detailed information on the role of guardians and how to be a guardian without running into legal trouble or family disputes.

## 3. Downsizing the Home

At some point, many parents move out of a larger home in which they raised their families and move into smaller accommodations. Most often, this happens after one parent is widowed. An aging parent may move into a long-term care facility, a smaller apartment or condominium, or into the home of one of his or her adult children. The choice of destination will depend on the mental and physical capabilities of the parent, as well as on the availability of the desired accommodation.

Although it is usually more economical for the parent to downsize, the reasons behind it are not just economic. Downsizing to a smaller place like a condominium or apartment can be an excellent solution for an aging parent who still has the mental and physical abilities needed to live alone. The parent is able to maintain the same level of independence and privacy he or she enjoyed before moving because he or she will still have a private residence, but will be free of physically demanding jobs such as shoveling snow, mowing grass, and heavy housework.

An additional bonus is that being in a secure apartment or condominium building where visitors have to be buzzed in and where there are security cameras in all public areas may provide the parent with more safety and security than he or she previously had when living in a house alone. Access to a trustworthy resident manager is also a benefit when a senior lives alone.

In many cases, when the large family home is sold, the proceeds of that sale will be used to buy the new, smaller place. There is usually some money left over to add to the resources available to support the parent, since the smaller place is almost always less expensive. In other cases, the proceeds of the sale of the family home are invested and used to pay for the parent's long-term care facility.

An issue that will come up when a parent downsizes to a smaller space is dealing with the furniture and personal possessions that are in the larger family home. Obviously there is not going to be room for everything in the new place and your parent is going to have to make some choices about what to keep and what to dispose. Be sensitive to the fact that this can be an upsetting process for many parents. Even though your parent might be suffering from memory loss or confusion, let him or her make as many choices and decisions as possible about what he or she wants to take to the new accommodations.

Remember that whenever a parent moves out of the family home into a newer place, it could be an emotional time for him or her. The family home is usually the repository of memories and reminders of his or her children and spouse, so leaving the home can be a sad experience for some parents. Once the idea of downsizing has been introduced, give your parent some time to get used to the idea of saying goodbye to the family home.

## 4. Move into Long-Term Care

For many families, moving an aging parent into a long-term care facility is really the only solution, but most feel that it is a last resort. This is partly due to the fact that parents almost universally resist the move. It is also partly due to the fact that the children of aging parents feel guilty about leaving a parent in an unknown place with strangers, particularly when the parent is making his or her unhappiness about the arrangement very clear. In fact, the guilt experienced when placing a parent in a long-term care facility is crippling for some people.

Always remember that when choosing a solution to the question of how and where your parent will live, the truly important question is whether any given solution is in the best interests of your parent. This does not mean that the solution you have found would necessarily be the best one; in an ideal world where money was no object, where your parent was perfectly healthy and you had all the time and energy in the world to devote to your parent. It means that it is the best solution that can be found given the circumstances in play at the time.

An important consideration is whether a move to a new place will cause the parent's condition (e.g., memory loss or confusion) to become worse. Because the parent's ability to adapt to new circumstances could already be impaired, some people are concerned that such a large change could accelerate deterioration. You may or may not be able to work around this concern; as mentioned above, for most people a long-term care facility is a last resort.

This is why a range of options have been set out in this chapter. If you place your parent in a long-term care facility, obviously you want to know that you have considered every reasonable option and that this is the best solution available to you.

Housing facilities for older people have changed quite a bit in recent years and all for the better. Now there are stages of housing that are designed to work with older individuals with different issues or shortcomings. Not all care facilities are the stereotypical nursing homes that were designed for people who have absolutely no ability to care for themselves at all. There is now an acknowledgement that there can be different levels of abilities. In many places you can choose the level of independence that is suitable.

For example, some facilities are designed as seniors' apartments, where each person lives in his or her own home in the building. There are benefits to this type of living, such as a building security and proximity to emergency health response teams. There are also other services available such as meal preparation, laundry, and housecleaning and the resident can choose the level of assistance that he or she wants. This tends to lead to peace of mind and comfort for a person who is still more or less independent but has trouble with one or two areas of daily living.

There are social benefits to moving into a seniors' facility too, such as more opportunities to interact with people rather than being isolated, and the availability of leisure and learning programs and activities.

Not all types of facilities are available everywhere, and even if they were, there is the matter of affording the care. However, before deciding that long-term care is or is not a solution for your family member, do your research and know what is available in your area, whether there is a long waiting list to get in, and what it will cost to live there. If cost is an issue, make sure you ask about any available government assistance.

Typically the choice of a care facility for a parent is a hotly debated topic at family meetings. Make sure you have current, accurate facts and not just outdated ideas or assumptions if your family is going to discuss it.

One of the questions that may be raised when discussing long-term care is whether your parent should be moved to a different geographical area. This is common when the parent does not live close to any of his or her children. If the parent is living somewhere where he or she is geographically distant from family, he or she is at risk of being (or feeling that he or she is being) isolated, abandoned,

or neglected. Keep in mind though, that moving a parent to a new city or town will mean separating the parent from his or her friends, familiar shopping areas, church or other place of worship, and familiar sights. As with most decisions that relate to aging parents, the right answer is always a balance of factors.

Ease the transition to a new facility by asking your parent which personal items he or she would like to take from home. There will not be room for much, as usually moving to a long-term care facility means moving into one bedroom and sharing common areas such as the dining room and TV room with the other residents. Therefore it is not likely to be possible to take large pieces of furniture, though you might make a point of taking one or two special pieces such as footstools or lamps.

You may also find that there is room to take a selection of framed photographs and pictures for the walls, as well as ornaments. When you move items to a facility, be aware of the possibility of them being misplaced, broken, or stolen.

If your parent is worried about what will happen with the rest of the furniture and personal items, do not dismiss the concern and say that you will look after it. A better idea is to offer to sit down with your parent and write down what he or she wants to see happen, such as giving specific items to certain family members, and do your best to carry out his or her wishes.

If your parent is not able to have this discussion due to confusion or memory loss, check his or her will to see whether he or she has made gifts of any household or personal items to anybody in particular. If so, you can carry out those gifts instead of more randomly giving away or selling household items. Be careful with this idea. It does not mean that you can help yourself to anything in your parent's home or allow others to do that. It just means that if there is simply no room for your parent's belongings any more and they must be disposed, it is better to dispose of them to the people your parent wants to benefit.

A request that aging parents frequently make at the time they are moving into a long-term care facility is that their home not be sold until they have had a chance to try the new facility. This seems to give them some reassurance that if the place is as bad as they think it is going to be, they can return home. This is another place where you have to be careful. On the one hand, almost everyone wants to give their parents the reassurance that they will hold off selling the home for a couple of weeks, and often they believe that saying so is an act of kindness. However, it is not at all fair to lead aging parents to believe that they can move back home again when you know that it simply is not possible.

If it is possible that your parent could live in his or her home again if other arrangements did not work, then by all means agree to hold on to the house for a set period of time to allow for a trial period. However, if it is simply never going to be possible, do not dishonestly make statements designed to trick your parent into complying with the move to long-term care.

Cost always has to be considered when you begin talking about moving a parent to long-term care. A particularly difficult situation exists when one parent has to move to long-term care but the other continues to live in the home. This means that the parents' incomes have to support what amounts to two households and this is often beyond the financial reach of seniors. Make sure you check into government assistance and insurance policies that might be in place.

# 5. Renovations to Your Parent's Home

Renovating your parent's home is a solution that is most appropriate for an older parent who still has the mental capacity to live independently, but has physical shortcomings. If your parent uses a wheelchair and his or her house is not set up to accommodate one, he or she simply cannot stay in the home without changes being made. However, these renovation suggestions are not restricted to individuals with wheelchairs; they are good ideas for any senior who lives alone.

These renovations might also have to be made to your home or that of one of your siblings if your parent is moving in with one of his or her children.

Some of the most common renovations include:

- Widening of doorways to accommodate a wheelchair.

- Lowering light switches for easy access for a person in a wheelchair.

- Adding an entryway ramp outdoors.

- Installing grab bars in showers and baths and perhaps in other areas of the house as well.

- Purchasing a shower seat.

- Installing a walk-in shower or bath rather than one entered by stepping over the side.

- Installing an anti-scald device on plumbing.

- Installing railings for outdoor stairs and porches.

- Installing elevators for indoor stairs.

- Converting to pullout shelves in the kitchen.
- Installing nonslip flooring and removing slippery area rugs, or replacing area rugs with rubber-backed rugs that will not slip.
- Installing rubber edges on steps and stairs.
- Installing windows that have easy-to-grip lever handles, that slide open easily, and that lock easily.
- Replacing small knobs on dressers, closets, medicine cabinets, and kitchen cupboards with larger ones that are easier to grasp.
- Replacing doorknobs with lever-style handles.
- Installing a telephone with large, easy-to-read numbers.
- Purchasing a hospital-style bed that can be adjusted for safety and comfort.

When helping an older parent with renovations, updates, or other changes to his or her home, be sure that you understand your parent's comfort level with technology. Some seniors are fluent in the current technology, but they are in the minority. It is not unusual to find older people who never turn on their televisions because they cannot figure out the remote and simply do not use gadgets such as cellular telephones or home-alarm systems. It can be quite dangerous for a senior to be home alone without access to a telephone.

Do not assume that because you are comfortable with any particular item of technology that your parent will be too. Many well-meaning children of seniors buy the latest items and when the parent objects, they simply say, "I'll show you how to use it." This does not often work out well. The senior often finds the writing or numbering on the device too small to read and is not familiar with certain symbols. Think about all of the symbols that appear across the top and bottom of your computer screen and consider how hard it would be to use your computer if you did not understand any of the symbols and somebody gave you one quick walk-through before leaving you with it.

You will not be able to force any technology on anyone who is not willing to learn it and work with it, nor should you try. Have an honest, heart-to-heart talk with your parent before you spend money on a laptop or BlackBerry for him or her.

## 6. Live-in Caregiver

If you have determined that your parent needs around-the-clock care or companionship, it is usually because your parent is still physically healthy but is suffering from increasing memory loss. An alternative to finding a long-term care facility in which your parent can live is finding an individual to live in your parent's home and act as a paid companion.

The success of this arrangement will depend on finding an appropriate person. This can be an overwhelmingly difficult search both for you and for your parent. Very few families have someone in the family who is available, willing, and able to provide this kind of care. You might find that your parent has an unreasonable idea that a particular family member should be the one to move in, regardless of the fact that the person he or she has chosen has other responsibilities such as a job or taking care of children.

You should realize that if your parent is fixating on someone in particular, it could well be that he or she feels that living with a stranger is dangerous or uncomfortable or an invasion of privacy. If your parent objects to a person you have chosen, try to find out specifically what the concern is. Sometimes there is no choice in the matter, but where possible, try to work with your parent's wishes.

You may also find it tough to find a person that you feel is trained, experienced, and compassionate enough to look after your parent. Many people worry about leaving a vulnerable parent alone with someone they do not really know well, even if that person was recommended by an agency. On top of the worry, there is also the same kind of guilt that many experience if they move a parent into long-term care.

If your parent is going to live alone or with a live-in caregiver, it is a good idea for you to place your parent's phone number on a national do-not-call registry. This will help to reduce the number of unsolicited sales calls made to your parent and therefore should help reduce the chances that your parent will be fooled by someone targeting seniors with a scam. Many seniors find high-pressure calls from strangers to be extremely stressful so reducing the calls should help reduce the stress.

# 7. Arrange for Paid Services

The services contemplated in this section are those that replace some of the work or activities that the aging parent used to do for himself or herself but now finds difficult to carry out. They include companies and individuals that will, for a fee, do the following:

- Clean the house
- Do yard work (e.g., raking, lawn mowing, tree pruning)
- Shovel snow
- Deliver groceries
- Deliver prescriptions

- Provide hot meals
- Drive seniors to appointments
- Walk dogs
- Repair and maintain the house (e.g., roof, plumbing, electrical, floors, windows, garage doors, sidewalk cracks)
- Move furniture or heavy objects
- Take discarded items to the dump

If you parent is unwell or is suffering from a loss of mental capacity, he or she might require more than this. You will have to decide how much care and assistance is needed, and monitor needs on an ongoing basis. The services in the previous list may be used in combination with in-home medical assistance such as nurses and nurse's aides who will help a senior with the following:

- Taking and organizing medications
- Taking injections
- Changing bandages
- Taking blood or urine samples
- Physiotherapy or therapeutic massage
- Measuring level of glucose, insulin, etc.
- Blood pressure reading
- Bathing, hair washing, oral hygiene, and grooming
- Transfer to and from a wheelchair
- Changing bed linens on a bed that is occupied by your parent
- Specialized medical care
- Palliative care

It might also be a good idea to hire someone who will act as a companion for your aging parent, particularly if geographic distance prevents you from visiting often and your parent has physical or mental disabilities. A companion is not a medical professional; he or she is more of a personal helper. Some of the jobs a companion might do include:

- Shopping for food, preparing meals, and cleaning up after meals.

- Changing bedding and towels.

- Doing the laundry.

- Light housekeeping.

- Getting your parent dressed, particularly for severe weather.

- Taking your parent to the library, shops, beauty salon, bank, post office, etc.

- Answering the door and telephone at your parent's house.

- Bringing in the mail and giving it to your parent.

- Making sure that your parent takes naps when needed.

- Helping your parent safely in and out of the bath, shower, bed, or wheelchair.

- Reading to your parent.

- Noticing when your parent needs new glasses, new gloves, a prescription refill, etc.

- Running small errands.

- Ensuring the security of the house such as locking doors, replacing smoke alarm batteries, and closing windows.

- Staying in regular contact with you and other family members.

- Generally seeing to the comfort of your parent by being present and attentive to his or her small needs.

Using an appropriate combination of these services may allow an aging parent to remain living in his or her home for a longer time than would otherwise be possible. This is important because most seniors do not want to leave behind the home where they lived their married lives and raised their children. If your parent, like so many others, tells you that he or she desperately wants to stay living in his or home, you will need to have an honest discussion with your parent to talk about what limitations exist now and those that are developing, and gather a team of people to help.

The downside of this arrangement is that it invites a series of strangers into the home of a senior who is alone. Having strangers in the home can be dangerous due to the fact that a senior can be very vulnerable, particularly when he or she is having memory lapses or confusion. You will have to be extremely careful when setting up these arrangements and should always supervise the workers and providers closely. Whenever possible, be present to greet workers or service providers to explain what is needed and confirm financial arrangements.

You might also find that even though you have selected and hired honest, hardworking people who pose no threat to the aging person, that aging person might still feel threatened by strangers in his or her home. It can be unbelievably stressful for a senior to answer the door to someone who expects to come in when the senior cannot remember who that person is. Think how you would feel if a complete stranger showed up at your home and started going through your things. It is not unusual for an aging parent to refuse to cooperate with or allow entry to service providers that family members have arranged and paid for.

## 8. Move in with Children

A common solution for many families is for an older parent, particularly when one is widowed, to move into the home of one of his or her children. As mentioned in Chapter 10, a survey called "Are Americans Talking with Their Parents about Independent Living?: A 2007 Study Among Boomer Women," done by the American Association of Retired Persons (AARP) in November, 2007, showed that 43 percent of respondents were considering the idea of having their older parent move in with them.

Sometimes there is a separate apartment or basement suite for the parent and in other cases the parent has only a bedroom to himself or herself and shares the house with the rest of the family.

The key to making this arrangement work is talking ahead of time. You might be surprised at how many problems and misunderstandings can be avoided by having one straightforward, honest conversation. This conversation is not a lecture by one person or a recitation of the rules of the house. It should be a chance for the parent and the adult child to talk about the assumptions they are making about the living arrangement and to try to envision what any given week would be like once the parent moves in. The goal is to make the transition go as smoothly as possible for all concerned and to head off future issues that might arise after the parent has moved in.

Ask your parent how he or she feels about moving into your home. On the one hand, while you might assume that your parent wants privacy, he or she might feel excluded and lonely sitting in the basement suite while you and your children watch television. On the other hand, you might assume that your parent wants to be included in everything, when in reality all he or she wants is some peace and quiet.

Talk about it, and make sure that everyone knows that this is a talk that is going to be relied on for making plans, so people need to be honest about what they want and do not want. This is not a time for the parent to be too polite to say that they find your children too noisy or that your household goes to bed too late at night.

Talk about exactly how the family operates. Try to find out whether it will be a good fit for your parent. Be specific about the rules of the house and your expectations of each other. For example, talk about whether your parent expects to do the following:

- Take every meal with the family or join only when invited.

- Do any chores and if so, which ones.

- Look after his or her own room.

- Act as a babysitter for your children.

- Have his or her own telephone line.

- Have his or her own private bathroom.

- Have his or her own private entrance.

- Come along on family vacations.

- Invite friends over whenever he or she wants.

- Borrow your car.

- Smoke in your house.

- Use your family computer and TV.

- Have his or her own pet.

Also discuss what your parent will expect of you and your family members who live with you. Your role will likely change over time if your parent should fall ill or suffer increased memory loss, but make sure everyone understands whether you will do the following:

- Always have someone in the house with the parent, even when you are at work.

- Provide meals, cleaning, or laundry.

- Take your parent to medical and dental appointments and pick up prescriptions.

- Make sure the house is quiet after a certain time at night.

- Allow your children to have their friends over when your parent is at home.

- Buy special foods or supplements for your parent.

- Renovate your home to better suit your parent.

- Accommodate your parent if you move to a new home in the future.

Also have a frank discussion about expenses. This should be brought up early on in the discussion process as it can be the source of a huge number of disputes. If your parent is expected to contribute to household bills, make sure that he or she knows that before making plans to move in. Agree on an amount and agree on how soon after moving in you and your parent will re-evaluate the amount to see if it is still reasonable. For example, it might be a good idea to sit down together after six months have passed to see whether your estimates of costs were accurate and whether any financial arrangements need to be tweaked.

Talk about how the expenses are going to be paid. You want to avoid a situation in which, for example, your parent picks up a bag of groceries as a contribution to the household, when you were expecting cash. That only leads to resentments over small things that tend to grow into large things.

Part of the discussion will also be with other family members so that you can get their input. Remember that everyone in the house is going to have to adjust to the reality that a new person is moving in, and it could well be a person who is going to need extra care and attention from everyone.

The fact that your parent is going to move in with you should not be a surprise to your siblings when it happens. Find out what kind of support each of them is prepared to offer. Also find out whether anyone has any objections to your parent living there and if so, whether their objections can be overcome. You may even find that one of your siblings wants your parent to live with them.

Consider putting a family care contract into place. There is more about this kind of contract in section **9.**

If you are planning to do any renovations to your home to accommodate your parent, such as putting in a wheelchair ramp, building a private entrance, or putting in new plumbing, make sure that this is also discussed at the family meeting. In most cases, a parent moving in with his or her children will require that some renovations take place to provide for safety and privacy (section **5.** discusses specific renovations that might be required).

Talk about who is paying for those renovations and who is overseeing the project. While it is fair that you should be reimbursed for any expenses you incur while preparing your home to suit your parent, it is a good idea to have your siblings onside with the idea before spending the money. Get written estimates before the work starts. Keep receipts to prove any expenditures that you might make from your parent's funds.

## 9. Family Care Contract

A family care contract, also known as a personal-care agreement or home-care agreement, is a formal, written agreement between a senior who needs care, and his or her family member who is prepared to provide care. These agreements are gaining in popularity across North

America. The idea is to clarify and set out just what the family member is going to do and how much he or she is going to be compensated for providing the services.

For example, if an older parent who is widowed is going to move in with her daughter, there could be a contract between them setting out what care the daughter is going to provide and what she will be paid. The contract might state, for example, that the daughter will provide full-time care, or that she will provide two or three hours a day. The time involved will depend on the care that is needed.

This idea is met with a whole range of emotions from both the parent and the caregiver. While on the surface it is purely a business arrangement, the fact that it involves a loved one makes it more complicated. You will have to decide whether it is right for your situation or not.

Some people are horrified and insulted at the very thought of being paid to look after their own parent. This insult, however, is one that most individuals cannot afford to take offence to. It costs money to add a person to your household, particularly a person who needs walking aids, prescriptions, and wheelchairs. More than that, the person giving the care must take extensive time away from work in most cases. This means the caregiver earns less money on the job, and has a shorter time in the workforce.

The end result is that there is less money to support the household and the caregiver's family, not to mention the caregiver's retirement when that time comes. Frankly, some people simply cannot afford to provide the care they would like to give their parent. In other words, it makes good financial sense to be paid to provide the services, and to clarify what the pay is going to be.

The caregiving services, if provided by a nonfamily member, would be paid for by the parent. To some people it seems that because the caregiver is a family member, the work should not be paid. The work is no less valuable when performed by a family member; in fact, it may be much higher in quality than that provided by a stranger. To refuse to let a family member be paid for looking after a parent would seem to say that the care of your parent is not valuable enough to warrant a wage.

The money is not free to the caregiver. The care becomes his or her job. He or she must declare the money earned under the contract as wages on his or her income tax return.

There are always benefits to having a mutually beneficial arrangement written down. The greatest advantage is that both sides are clear on what is going to happen, when it is going to happen, who is going to do what, and when the arrangement is going to end. This eliminates assumptions and expectations that may not have been thought of by the other party, thereby cutting down on disappointments and disputes.

The clarification benefits the parent and the caregiver, but it helps others in the family as well. Siblings and other family members often wonder, either to themselves or out loud, just how much that caregiver is getting from the parent. Having an agreement that other family members can look at will help them understand the arrangement and possibly to understand that when the parent passes away, there might not be much left over for any of them to inherit. It is better that they be aware of this financial arrangement as it happens than to disappoint them at the time the parent dies and have to go through an estate dispute.

Some of the items that must be clarified under the agreement include:

- When the services are going to start.

- How long the services will be provided.

- That either the parent or the caregiver can end the contract when he or she wants.

- The kinds of services that are going to be given (e.g., housekeeping, nursing, companionship, transportation, meals, personal hygiene).

- How much the caregiver will be paid and whether it will be hourly, weekly, etc.

A key to this arrangement being valid is that the parent must have legal mental capacity to deal with financial documents if he or she is going to sign a contract.

If you are contemplating a family care contract, bring it up at your family meeting and let each family member ask their questions and give their opinions. If you find that there is a great deal of resistance to the idea, it might be a good idea to calculate what it would cost to have outside caregivers or agencies provide the services you are prepared to provide, and to give those numbers to your family members.

## 10. Representation Agreement

The representation agreement is a solution that differs from a health-care directive in one very important way; it appoints a chosen person to make decisions *with* the aging parent as opposed to *for* the aging parent. It is a cooperative arrangement that is put into writing.

A representation agreement is not available everywhere, as not all jurisdictions have passed laws that allow this arrangement. Where it is available, and where the parent in question retains enough mental capacity to participate in decision making, it can be very useful.

The representation agreement formalizes the legal relationship so that the older person knows whom he or she can and should rely on for assistance. It also tells the rest of the world, including concerned family members, medical personnel, and caregivers, that the aging person has made a choice as to who is allowed to give some help.

This kind of agreement is generally used only for health and personal decisions, and not financial decisions.

# Conclusion

At the end of this chapter and on the CD that accompanies this book, you will find a form called Identify the Right Solutions for Your Family. The worksheet will help you to identify which of the many solutions identified in previous chapters are likely to apply to your parents and your family situation.

There are two ways to use this worksheet. One is to take it to your family meeting and to work through it as a group. This is ideal if you want to give some structure to the meeting and make it clear which way your family should be going. Using the worksheet might help prevent you and your family members from getting that feeling of being overwhelmed by too many unfamiliar options.

The second way to use the worksheet is to work through it with your parents without help or input from other family members. You will find that this will give quite a different outcome, since the first question on the worksheet has to do with capacity.

The worksheet operates by eliminating choices or solutions that do not apply to you and by streamlining you into checklists that do apply. The first question, as mentioned, has to do with whether or not your parents still have mental capacity to do their own planning, because this is one of the pivotal facts in any estate planning. If your parents no longer have mental capacity, a number of options are eliminated and you will have to take different steps.

If your answer to the first question is that your parents do in fact have capacity, you will be directed into Stream 1. If you say they do not have capacity, you will be directed into Stream 2.

Once you have finished reading this book and have completed the worksheet, you will have a tailored list of solutions. You can then go back to Chapters 12 and 13 to reread the solutions that apply to you.

You can complete the worksheet separately for each parent if you wish. This is definitely a good idea where both parents are doing their planning, but one parent is healthier, either physically or mentally, than the other.

SAMPLE 3
# IDENTIFY THE RIGHT SOLUTIONS FOR YOUR FAMILY

**Question 1:**
Does your parent now have the mental capacity necessary to understand and sign legal documents?

☐ Yes — go to Stream 1 below
☐ No — go to Stream 2 below

If you are not sure if your parent has mental capacity or not, see section **1.1** in Chapter 1 of the book for help. You can also get help from your parent's family doctor or a doctor who specializes in geriatrics, in the form of an assessment of your parent's abilities.

| Stream 1 | | Stream 2 | |
|---|---|---|---|
| Yes, my parent has the mental capacity necessary to understand and sign legal documents. | | No, my parent does not have the mental capacity necessary to understand and sign legal documents. | |
| **Question 2:** Does your parent have a will, an enduring power of attorney, and a health-care directive already in place? | | **Question 2:** Does your parent have a will, an enduring power of attorney, and a health-care directive already in place? | |
| ☐ Yes — go to 1A below and use only that column<br>☐ No — go to 1B below and use only that column | | ☐ Yes — go to 2A below and use only that column<br>☐ No — go to 2B below and use only that column | |
| **1A** | **1B** | **2A** | **2B** |
| Yes my parent has mental capacity and already has a will, an enduring power of attorney, and a health-care directive in place. | No my parent has mental capacity but does not have a will, an enduring power of attorney, or a health-care directive in place. | Yes my parent does not have mental capacity but does have a will, an enduring power of attorney, and a health-care directive in place. | No my parent does not have mental capacity and does not have a will, an enduring power of attorney, and a health-care directive in place. |

| | | | |
|---|---|---|---|
| This situation has the greatest range of options available. Financial solutions available include:<br><br>• Put assets in joint names<br>• Set up a bare trust<br>• Change his or her will<br>• Set up an *inter vivos* trust<br>• Set up a custody account<br>• Prepare a business succession plan<br>• Sell his or her business<br>• Designation of beneficiaries on plans and policies<br>• Representation agreement | Financial solutions available include all of the financial solutions listed in 1A plus:<br><br>• Make a will and an enduring power of attorney | Financial solutions available to the person acting as power of attorney on behalf of the parent include:<br><br>• Sell the home<br>• Sell the business<br>• Set up a custody account | This situation has the least options available. Financial solutions available include:<br><br>• Court-appointed trustee<br><br>Once appointed by the court, a trustee may:<br><br>• Set up a custody account<br>• Sell the business<br>• Sell the family home and/or cottage |
| Nonfinancial solutions available include:<br><br>• Downsize from family home<br>• Live in long-term care (if there are physical limitations)<br>• Renovate the home to continue to live there<br>• Hire a live-in caregiver<br>• Receive paid services in the home<br>• Move in with one of the children<br>• Family care contract | Nonfinancial solutions available include all of the nonfinancial options under 1A plus:<br><br>• Make a health-care directive | Nonfinancial solutions available to the agent acting under the health-care directive on behalf of the parent include:<br><br>• Downsize from family home<br>• Live in long-term care<br>• Renovate the home to continue to live there<br>• Hire a live-in caregiver<br>• Receive paid services in the home<br>• Move in with one of the children | Nonfinancial solutions available include:<br><br>• Court-appointed guardian<br>• Once the guardian is appointed, all of the nonfinancial options listed in 2A are available to the guardian |